T21

TALL MEN WITH
LONG RIFLES

THE BATTLE OF SAN JACINTO

TALL MEN WITH LONG RIFLES

*The Glamorous Story of the Texas Revolution,
As Told by Captain Creed Taylor, Who
Fought in That Heroic Struggle
From Gonzales to San
Jacinto.*

Set Down and Written Out By

JAMES T. DeSHIELDS

Author of

"The Presidents and Governors of Texas"
"The Men Who Made Texas"
"Border Wars of Texas"
"I am Houston"
Etc.

⊷{ ILLUSTRATED }⊶

SAN ANTONIO, TEXAS
THE NAYLOR COMPANY
1935

Copyright, 1935 by
THE NAYLOR COMPANY

Printed in the United States of America
All rights reserved. This book, or
parts thereof, may not be reproduced
in any form without permission of
the publisher.

Patriotism comes with the love of country. That love is kindled and kept alive through history. To all who would know more of the matchless history of Texas and its heroic patriots, this volume is DEDICATED.

FOREWORD

The story of the Texas Revolution will always thrill, will kindle the spark of patriotism. The Alamo, Goliad, and San Jacinto will ever remain shrines of liberty for the lovers of heroism and freedom to worship. Ours was certainly the most heroic struggle for liberty in all American history; and it is indeed fitting that a great Centennial celebrates the first hundred years of free Texas.

The story is a glamorous, swift-moving one—from Gonzales to San Antonio, and on to the glorious victory on the field of San Jacinto—and the heroes of that valiant struggle introduce themselves in such rapid gallant style. Here pass in review Stephen F. Austin, Colonel John Moore, Old Ben Milam, Deaf Smith, Henry Karnes, Fannin, Bowie, Burleson, Johnson, Travis, Crockett, Bonham, Sherman, Lamar, Lane, Sam Houston, and many others in that radiant galaxy of immortal heroes.

Creed Taylor was one of the most notable men who played a part in the heroic age of Texas, a man of heroic mould who played a hero's part in a heroic drama. This valiant soldier was a gift of Tennessee to Texas—one of that buckskin clad, rifle armed little army who fought for and won the Texas of today.

To hear history from those who helped make it, is always interesting, because of its realism and its adherence to truth. History-minded people should welcome this volume as a treasure to be added to their store of Texas historical lore. This work tells of the epic age of Texas, and is unique, since it is the only complete personal narrative of the Texas Revolution that has come down to posterity. Those old Texans were fighters, not writers, more adept with rifle than pen. Rough, unlettered, their style was not very ornate, but their narratives bear the stamp of truth, and carry an interest that stilted history does not possess.

A few years before the grizzled old veteran, Creed Taylor passed away, he was induced to dictate his recollections of the Texas War of Independence; and in prefacing his narrative, said: "I may not be capable of posing as a historian; but having personal knowledge of most of the stirring episodes transpiring in the course of our fight for liberty, I shall attempt to tell the story of my part in that glorious struggle."

Through legends, garnered by careless, periphrastic writers, many errors have crept into Texas history and gained credence. The narrator, from personal knowledge, has corrected many such false statements, and thrown new light upon many mooted incidents in our matchless annals. *Creed Taylor was there; he wrote what he saw and knew.* From such sources has come this colorful epic of the heroic age of Texas. The story thrills.

Roll back the scroll of time for a century! The clock of destiny strikes! The time is the eventful year of 1835, the place is the province of Texas. A great drama is to be staged; the actors are training for their parts and jostling in the wings for place—they are TALL MEN WITH LONG RIFLES!

Dallas, Texas

April 21, 1935   JAMES T. DeSHIELDS

NOTE

In presenting Creed Taylor's personal reminiscences of the Texas Revolution, the writer has sought to edit and arrange the material in such a manner as to retain the spontaneity and vitality of the narrator's own colorful style, and yet relieve the reader from the confusion of repetitive and irrelevant matter. The accounts have been further clarified by the inclusion of corroborative information drawn from many reliable sources. The field of view is thus broadened, and the interpretations are at once both authentic and convincing. The purpose of the writer has been well attained. The narrative is interesting and illuminating.

THE PUBLISHERS

PRELUDE

(How the "Tall Men with Long Rifles" came)

On the first day of the year 1822, one of the most memorable scenes of that colorful tapestry which is Texas history, was woven. A little band of sturdy Americans had crossed the Red River, and now, penetrating into the Spanish domain of Texas, began a hazardous trek. Day by day the little caravan trudged across the primitive wilderness, cutting paths through the trackless forest, rafting over swollen streams, but dauntless, on and on they pressed, deeper and deeper into the wild strange country.

In advance of the serpentine line of covered wagons carrying the women and children with scanty supplies of household goods, rode "Tall Men with Long Rifles." They were the invincible type of pioneers that had carried civilization across the continent, into the Middle West, the South, and now —into the far Southwest!

On the last day of the year 1821, the weary migrants reached the Brazos, crystalline Texas stream, and the prospect that greeted their eyes was inviting. "In the beginning" this stream had been the goal to which the early explorers had aspired. The romantic Spaniards named it "Brazos de Dios" (Arm of God). Now, years after, it was the goal of these venturesome American immigrants, who would linger here to conceive a new nation.

Ere the brave little band of pioneers had crossed the Brazos and started further on their journey, a new year had dawned. With that dawn came a new era in Texas history. With the fiery rising sun a history, just as fiery, was begun.

On a beautiful little tributary of the river, camp was pitched and a permanent settlement started. Other sturdy settlers followed in the wake of these valorous pioneers, and thus began the American wave of settlement in Texas.

Soon a village sprang up on the banks of the Brazos. Its founders were descendants of those patriots who generously spilled their blood in the American Revolution. Thus the village derived its name, Washington.

Here, in this historic hamlet, a few years later, thronged another band of fearless men, who wisely deliberating, boldly declared Texas a free republic! Came War! And came TALL MEN WITH LONG RIFLES!

TABLE OF CONTENTS

Foreword		ix
Prelude		xiii

Chapter		Page
I.	The Fires of Revolt Blaze on the Frontier	1
II.	Tall Men with Long Rifles Ride into the Fray	9
III.	The Flags of War Fly as Houston Arrives	22
IV.	Famous Fighters March Upon San Antonio	33
V.	Burleson Commands as the Quasi-Siege Begins	43
VI.	Who'll Go with Old Ben Milam into Bexar?	51
VII.	Milam Meets His Death in the Texan Victory	57
VIII.	Dr. Grant and his Matamoros Expedition Starts Trouble	71
IX.	An Expedition Without a Parallel in American Warfare	83
X.	The Fathers of Texas in August Assembly	92
XI.	The Great Runaway Scrape	102
XII.	"By the Eternal We Are Going to Win, or Die!"	114
XIII.	Bowie, Crockett, Travis, Bonham Pass in Review	134
XIV.	The Most Heroic Fight in American History	151
XV.	Santa Anna Vows to Exterminate the Texans	170
XVI.	A Famous Hero Comes Upon the Scene	180
XVII.	Fannin Gambles with Fate—And Loses	193
XVIII.	The Greatest Day in Texas History	211
XIX.	Tragedy and Humor Stalk the Field of San Jacinto	226
XX.	From Camp-fire to Hearth-stone	234

ILLUSTRATIONS

The Battle of San Jacinto	Frontispiece

	Opposite Page
Karnes Leads the Attack with a Crowbar	61
Travis Draws the Line in the Alamo	146
Crockett is the Last Survivor of the Alamo	161
The Massacre at Goliad	195
Santa Anna Before Houston at San Jacinto	228

TALL MEN WITH LONG RIFLES

CHAPTER I

The Fires of Revolt Blaze on the Frontier

Texas is the only state of the American Union that was once a free Republic, and she maintained that proud position for a period of ten years, voluntarily surrendering her sovereignty for a place in the galaxy of the greatest Republic on earth.

The "Lone Star" Republic was one of the most unique nations of the world, and its career furnishes some of the most glamorous pages of American history. That was the heroic period of Texas history, and it is indeed appropriate that the state should celebrate the first hundred years of its existence in the calendar of time in a great and patriotic Centennial Exposition.

The Texas Revolution was one of the most heroic wars in all history—a struggle carried on to final triumph against a powerful nation of eight million souls, by a pioneer community of less than thirty thousand people, and with a mere handful of buck-skin clad, rifle-armed frontiersmen, without treasure or training and under the most adverse conditions: As a soaring orator once exclaimed, "The Republic of Texas was capitalized with less men and money, but with more patriotism and gallantry than any nation on earth."

Once the tides of revolution against Mexico set in, they moved rapidly and surely toward that event. The history of Texas throughout is a glamorous one; but a more heroic one is now to be ushered in. The hands of time on the clock of destiny have moved around to that eventful year of 1835. A crisis has arrived in the affairs of Texas. Henceforward the stream of her history is to widen and flow with swifter current. The gestures of the Mexican military have caused the American colonists of the province to rise and arm for actual war. Comes war! The Texas Revolution of 1835-1836 was as logical, as inevitable as the American Revolution of 1775-1776. Only half a century had passed and many veterans of that war still lived, some in Texas. Recollections of that heroic first struggle for freedom on American soil were fresh in the memory of many men.

"As a boy," says Creed Taylor, "of course I did not understand about 'ulterior causes and world politics' that our historians tell us lead up to the war. It might have been the persistent efforts of the 'greedy American land-grabbers' to take Texas away from Mexico. I always understood that the Fredonian Revolt, was launched for that express purpose. That futile affair, occurring as far back as 1826, was however premature and ill-starred. It, at least, served to kindle the smouldering fires of hate and was really a forerunner of what actually happened ten years later. Father often said that Texas would not long 'stand hitched,' that the Americans would rise in arms, whip Mexico, and own Texas. Many brave and patriotic characters were drifting in and with their bold gestures, the spirit of resistance to Mexican tyranny grew and the determination to be free took deep root.

"It used to be said that 'Old Hickory' Jackson claimed Texas rightly belonged to the United States, and that it should be *reannexed;* that if he could not get the country back with 'gold and silver' he could take it with 'powder and lead.'

"At one time it was current report that a man

named Sam Houston, a big white chief of the Indians'—was getting up a great force of painted warriors to invade Texas and take the country away from Mexico. That was the first I ever heard of Houston, and I was told he was a 'Big Captain.' Many of the settlers knew this remarkable man, and were anxious that he should come and help them in their struggle for liberty. The first time I ever saw General Houston was at our army camp on the Cibolo, in October, 1835, after the war had opened and I admit I had expected to see a man actually in the regalia of an Indian war chief. He was however, a picturesque enough figure, and I can never forget the incident of that occasion.

"Texas was then the Eldorado of America, and many bold and worthy young fellows were constantly coming into the new 'land of promise.' And right here I want to resent the erroneous idea that long prevailed to the effect that the early Texans were a 'tough and lawless bunch.' That early population was composed of the best and bravest pioneers of the period. There were, of course some lawless and desperate characters among them, especially about the old Mexican settlements of Nacogdoches, in the redlands along the Louisiana-Texas border, and about San Antonio; but the greater bulk of the colonists, especially those of Austin's colony, were a peaceful, industrious, and worthy people. They belonged to that type of men who won the battles of civilization over and against the savages of the Middle West, in Kentucky, Tennessee, Louisiana, expanding the limits of the Great Republic from the Alleghenies to the Mississippi, and thence by their intrepid daring, amid difficulties and dangers without precedent or parallel, to the golden valleys of California, and the blue waters of the Pacific. Whatever of vice or crime may have stained some individual careers were the sins of vital impulses and primal passions. There were no degenerates among them, for by inheritance and association they were the sons of the frontier, of whom it has been truly said: 'The cowards never started and the weaklings died on the way.'

"Among those who came to the new land of opportunity during the Colonial Period, was a most gallant and worthy young fellow, no less a personage than William Barrett Travis, destined to play a most colorful and important part in the tumultuous affairs of Texas and to win immortal fame. This dauntless hero and martyr to liberty is entitled to at least brief mention in this connection. The facts in his brief career are meager. It is known that Travis was born in the Edgefield district, South Carolina, August 9, 1809, the eldest of seven children born to Mark Travis and wife, Jemima Stallworth Travis; that he removed with his parents to Conecuh County, Alabama, in 1818 and there assisted in clearing and putting into cultivation a large farm, yet known as the 'Travis place.'

"Denied the privileges of attending school in his boyhood years, he was taught the elementary essentials of education by his mother. He later attended the Evergreen Academy which was founded and conducted by his uncle, the Rev. Alexander Travis. He then studied law under Hon. James Dillett, at Claiborne, Alabama, and was licensed to practice. He was a large, handsome man, of florid complexion, a gifted speaker, and soon became a very able lawyer.

"Domestic troubles seem to have shattered his brilliant prospects and sent him to the new land of Texas. While a law student he had married a handsome young lady of Claiborne, and to this union two children, a boy nd a girl, were born. The separation occurred in 1831, and Travis immediately left for Texas, carrying with him one of the family servants, a negro man named Ben. The faithful slave remained with his master to the end. Some two years after the Texas war he returned to the Travis family in Alabama, and often, always with tear-dimmed eyes and quivering lips, the old darky would relate the tragic story of the Alamo fight, and how he had witnessed the death "right thar before my eyes" of "Moster Willum," pierced by many bullets as he exposed himself in firing the last—the very last—cannon shot from the Alamo."

"Bill Travis, as he was called by his friends, was a flaxen-haired, blue-eyed, chivalrous looking young man of fine physique, dignified looking, standing six feet tall and weighing one hundred and seventy five pounds. Under ordinary conditions he was mild mannered enough but when stirred up his fighting ire rose and reached a high pitch. He was a bold, frank, and courageous man, engaging and attractive in his manners, but perfectly fearless and outspoken, which trait he did not fail to exhibit in his comments upon the high-handed and arbitrary course of the Mexican military authorities sent into the province to overawe and rule the liberty-loving American colonists.

"Most of the troops sent into Texas were *Presidarios*—a term applied to all convict soldiers. Hence the garrisons in the provinces were composed of convicts, the vilest class of criminals the ratero slums of Mexico could produce. These murderous thieves and ex-highwaymen, offsprings of a debased race, were foisted upon the American settlers of Texas to overawe, and to hold them in subjection to the tyranny of Comandante Bustamente.

"And here I shall relate an incident of minor importance within itself, but which came near resulting in an actual clash of arms and which helped to kindle the fires of revolt that finally flared up into flame and produced the actual revolution some four or five years later. Some of our historians briefly mention this affair, but none of them give any particulars. It was a matter of much gossip among the settlers at the time, and the story makes interesting reading.

"Quite a number of Americans had settled in and around Anahuac, and one afternoon in 1831 while four *presidarios* of the garrison were prowling around, they entered the house of a settler, and finding the husband away and the wife alone, attempted a heinous, but nameless crime—the brave woman beating off her assailants until timely help chanced to come. The woman fought with the fury of a demon and her loud screams attracted the attention of a small party hunting in the vicinity, who rushed to the scene. When they reached the house they found the door securely fastened on the inside and a terrible struggle going on within. Without a moments hesitation they seized heavy timbers, broke open the door, and rushed upon the demons. Three of the miscreants fled and escaped. The fourth, who according to the lady's testimony was the ring leader, was knocked down and securely bound. As news of the affair spread, a posse gathered at the scene. All were highly wrought and some of them wanted to hang the wretch to the nearest limb; one or two suggested that the fiend's head be cut off and hoisted on a pole in view of the fort. But wiser council prevailed—the prisoner was a soldier of the republic, and such a course would be an insult to the flag; the Mexican authorities would use it as a pretext to inflict greater tyranny against the colonists. But they would inflict such punishment as would serve as a warning to his thieving, cut-throat comrades.

"A bucket of tar was procured and a heavy coating was applied to the culprit from head to foot. Then, with her own hands still bleeding from the effects of her terrible fight, the lady ripped open her feather bed and the trembling wretch was given an ornate dressing of feathers. He was then mounted astride a rail, and in this garb and manner was carried through the settlement and village, and finally turned loose near the fort with a message for Bradburn to the effect that should such another outrage be committed or attempted by his convict gang, the Texans would rise to a man, and that not even a *pelado* would be left to black the commander's boots.

"Among those concerned in this embroglio was the fearless young patriot, Bill Travis, and with him chanced to be such other patriotic and daring fellows as Patrick C. Jack, Sam T. Allen, and Monroe Edwards—that was before Edwards had developed into a notorious celebrated forger. When Bradburn learned of this affair he flew into a towering rage and swore that every one concerned in the matter would be arrested for insulting the flag by outraging a soldier of the government, and sent in chains to Vera Cruz for trial before a military court.

"The arrest of Travis and his comrades was the spark that set off the flame. The news flew over the country like wild fire and created the highest indignation. Mass meetings were held in various communities; one assembled at Brazoria on December 16, 1831, and presided over by the fiery patriot, Branch T. Archer, was of a very bold and revolutionary nature. Needless to say the prisoners were soon set at liberty, but the spirit of revolt began to flare up everywhere and was soon at white heat. History tells all about the stirring scenes and thrilling events that followed—till the final clash came.

"But no matter all this. All I knew or cared for was that a big fuss was on hand and that men were needed to fight. I thought I could shoot Mexicans as well as I could shoot Indians, or deer, or turkeys; and so, with an older brother, Josiah, and several other young fellows of our neighborhood—'all armed to the teeth'—I rode away to war."

CHAPTER II

Tall Men with Long Rifles Ride Into the Fray

"The first or opening scrap of the War—it could hardly be called a battle—occurred at Gonzales, on October 2, 1835; and in this way. Some time previously the Mexican Commandante at Bexar had loaned or given to the settlers of that exposed outpost an old brass cannon for protection against the Indians. This old gun, as I afterwards learned, had been spiked and the spike bored out, leaving a touch hole as large as an ordinary gun barrel and as a weapon of defense was almost worthless other than to make a loud noise when fired and that was quite effective when used upon a bunch of prowling redskins. The Mexican authorities knew that the gun was practically worthless, but they wanted a pretext for beginning hostilities, and so they sent Capt. Castenado with a company of soldiers, over to Gonzales with a preemptory demand for the surrender of the cannon, and the threat to take it by force if necessary.

"Captain Albert Martin was the spokesman for the citizens; and he resorted to a bit of strategy by parleying and playing for time until he could send out fast riding messengers, calling on the settlers of the surrounding country to hasten to his aid. Well do I remember the incident when a rider on a foaming steed dashed up to our house, told of the trouble at Gonzales town, and then spurred on to spread the news. And everywhere men volunteered and hastened forward to help their friends. The war was on, and 'tall men' with 'long rifles' were hastening forward ready for the fray.

"At Bastrop a small company was organizing with the noted Ranger chief, Robert Colemen, as

TALL MEN WITH LONG RIFLES

Captain and John Tumlinson as First-Lieutenant, and I promptly enlisted. I was now a real soldier. Recruits came in rapidly, and in a very short time our company had its full complement of men. Marching out with much pomp and pride, we reached the 'seat of war,' Gonzales, on the last day of September, and found there a force of about one hundred men and boys, all volunteers, who had hurriedly responded to the call to arms and were eager to fight. With recruits arriving almost hourly, things began to take on a war-like appearance. 'Tall Men with Long Rifles' were in evidence everywhere and 'ready to fight at the drop of the hat'.

"Early the next morning the restless volunteers were ordered to parade for inspection. They presented an appearance strangely in contrast with the gaily uniformed 'dude' soldiers one may see on dress parade at fairs and military reviews of the present day. Every man carried a long flint-lock, muzzle-loading rifle, with shot pouch and powder horn. Most of the men wore buck-skin breeches and hunting shirts or jackets, and these garments, from wear and exposure, presented a variety of colors, from a bright yellow to a glossy black, and as to head-gear every style was in evidence, from the coonskin cap to the high-crowned 'sombrero.' Nearly all wore shoes, some moccasins, and these were handmade from home-tanned leather. Boots were then not much in vogue, and I believe I am safe in saying there was not a pair in the army at Gonzales; in fact, the only pair of boots I remember seeing during the campaign were worn by General Houston when he visited the army on the Cibolo. All the men carried large knives in a sheath attached to their belts and some carried pistols of various patterns, fashioned after the ideas of local gunsmiths of that day. Occasionally one would see a double-barrelled pistol, but these were rare, nearly all being of the single-barrelled type and were either carried at the belt or in a holster at the horn of the saddle.

"When the boys were drawn up in line the old pioneer preacher, W. P. Smith, made a patriotic and rousing speech, reciting the wrongs we had suffered, as he would point to the smoke ascending from the camp of the Mexicans just across the river. This speech aroused the boys to such a pitch that it required the restraint of older heads to prevent them from making an immediate onslaught upon the invaders. They were at a high pitch and anxious for a fight.

"One man in the throng was especially conspicuous and, if possible, he seemed more eager for the fray than any other. This was old Martin Palmer, 'the ring-tailed panther'—a soubriquet he acquired while serving as a member of the territorial legislature of Missouri, during a free-for-all fight among members on one occasion.

"The 'Panther,' as he was called, was a Virginian, and a typical backwoodsman, who had spent most of his life along the frontiers of Kentucky, Tennessee, Missouri, Arkansas, and Texas, and had much notoriety throughout the southwest as a fighter and hunter. But some of his wonderful exploits must have been exaggerated, if not pure fabrications. As a hunter, he was, perhaps, the equal of Davy Crockett, and in stealth and cunning he must have been a close second to Daniel Boone or the Wetzels. It is said that when his favorite bear dog died Palmer much grieved, actually had a minister come fifty miles through the wilderness to deliver a funeral oration over the grave of the canine. Another story illustrates his way of meting out justice. An Osage Indian had wantonly slain a white man, a friend of Palmer's, and had cut out and eaten the heart of his victim—from which fact he was called 'Two Hearts.' The 'Panther' planned revenge, and feigning friendship, invited the fiendish savage to a feast and bidding him partake freely, stood over his guest with a drawn bowie-knife compelling him to eat until he actually died.

"Palmer was one of the leaders of the Freedonian Revolt, signing that compact and commanding the small force of about fifty militia that rallied to the support of that forlorn movement. It was said that Palmer supplied historian Yoakum with the data for his account of this affair. Palmer was also one of the signers of the Declaration of Independence of March 2, 1836, a true patriot, and he took part in all the revolutionary movements of that early period and rightly his memory is perpetuated in the name of one of the counties of Texas.

"Though illiterate and rough mannered Palmer was a man of more than ordinary parts, of most extraordinary strength of mind and body and brave as a lion. He was of large stature and bronzed of feature, always dressed in buckskin hunting shirt and leather trousers, with a panther skin cap, wore his hair long and platted in Indian style, and was indeed a unique figure. I first saw the 'Panther' at our home on Taylor's Bayou and he impressed me as a most extraordinary character. As a boy I was fascinated with the marvelous stories of his exploits and adventures with red men and with wild animals.

"On this occasion the 'Panther' was well mounted and armed, and in high glee, eager for a brush with the enemy; as he expressed it, 'just itching and clawing for a scrap with the cowardly 'greasers'.

"Of leaders on this occasion there was no dearth. John A. Wharton, John H. Moore, William H. Jack, James Fannin, Albert Martin, J. E. W. Wallace, John Hensley, Captain Alley, and others whose later achievements gave them immortal renown, were present and were willing to lead us to victory or to a shallow grave. There seemed to be considerable rivalry among these heroes as to who should have the leadership of the little army, and when the vote was taken that morning, while on parade, Col. John H. Moore, the old Ranger Chief and Indian fighter, was elected to the chief command, and J. E. W. Wallace was made second in authority.

"I well remember the fine martial appearance of our commander, looking every inch a soldier. He was one of the 'Old Guard' Ranger chiefs and had won his spurs as a gallant fighter in numerous fierce combats with Indians on the frontier.

"It is said that Col. Moore first visited Texas about the time the redoubtable Dr. James Long made his unfortunate venture into the province, declaring Texas a free Republic and setting up his ephemeral government at Nacogdoches. That bold stroke occurred back in 1818-1819, and grew out of the Aaron Burr scheme, and was really the first attempt to make Texas a free republic. The bold gesture forms one of the glamorous chapters of early day Texas history.

"We know that Col. Moore came as one of Austin's 'Original Three Hundred' in 1821, settling permanently at a point on the Colorado River, where he later founded the beautiful town of La Grange. He was born in Tennessee on the first day of the nineteenth century. His father was a son of the 'dark and bloody ground,' and his mother was a native of the 'Old Dominion,' so it was but natural that the son should become a famous border fighter. He was a staunch patriot, and one of the earliest and most zealous advocates of Texas independence, being one of the proscribed leaders whose arrest was ordered by General Cos in 1835. He was truly one of the 'tall' men who helped to make Texas. During the years of the Republic he commanded a company of Rangers. His great battle and victory over the Comanches on the Red Fork of the Colorado, and far out on the frontier in October, 1840, virtually broke the back-bone of that powerful and warlike tribe in Texas.

"After the selection of our commander, we were ordered to our quarters and told to hold ourselves in readiness for action upon a moment's notice.

"It may be in order to state just here that our little army was organized for fighting, but nothing else. We had no commissary, no quartermaster, no medical corps, although there were several physicians present, and this matter was spoken of but as being unimportant, no baggage train and not even a flag, but this latter was provided a few days later, as we shall relate. The ammunition, rifle balls with bullet moulds, an extra flint or two, gun wiper and 'bullet patchin' were carried by each man in his 'shot pouch' made of leather or dressed skins and worn at the side suspended by a broad strap that went over the shoulder. Attached to this pouch was the powder horn. Thus on the morning of October 1st, 1835, was accoutred that little army, the hope of a new nation. It was not formidable in numbers and it may not have had a very martial appearance, but it was *our army* and to all intents and purposes it was as invincible as Caesar's legions or the 'Old Guard' of Napoleon.

"Of rations we had an abundance. Corn was plentiful, the gardens were full of fresh vegetables, while fat cattle were to be found on the prairies. All of these things were freely offered to us by the citizens of Gonzales, and during our stay of nearly two weeks we fared as well as the best appointed army of modern times.

"The Mexican force lay in camp on the opposite

or south side of the river and their picket guards could be seen from the town. Castenado was all this while waiting a reply from Captain Martin as to whether he would give up the cannon. Martin had shrewdly evaded a final answer under one pretext or another, in order to gain time in which to rally the Texans to his relief. This accomplished, on Thursday evening Col. Moore ordered us into line and in a few words told us that he considered our force sufficient to defeat the enemy and that he proposed to attack at once. He stated that in order to ascertain the approximate strength of the Mexican forces he decided to advance a company of men in the direction of the Mexican camp as a feeler. To this end fifty mounted men crossed the river, followed by the main command as infantry, leaving their horses in town under strong guard. The Gonzales men, with the aid of the others, had constructed a rude sort of fort with a trussed top upon which was mounted the coveted cannon, a small company under Lieut. Almaron Dickenson, who afterwards fell in the Alamo, being appointed to serve the piece. Of course we all felt proud of our 'artillery,' mainly for two reasons: it was the bone of contention; the Mexicans came for it and had said they were not going back without it, and by placing it in a conspicuous place in the battle line we thought it would serve to nerve them on and by that means give us a chance to humble their pride in open fight. We also cherished the idea that loaded as it was, with slugs and scrap iron, when once fired at close range it would carry slaughter into the ranks of the enemy, and those not killed outright would probably be scared off the field.

"When the mounted men crossed the river they were halted a short distance from the crossing and held in position until the remainder of our forces had crossed, after which they pushed forward until they came within full view of the Mexicans. Their pickets fired upon the advancing column and it was only through an effort on the part of the officers that those men were held in check. They wanted to charge the 'greasers' and teach them a lesson then and there. This was about sundown on the first of October and instead of advancing upon the enemy, as we had expected, we were ordered to rest on our arms until morning. This was entirely 'against the grain' with most of us as we had left our blankets in town and only a few of the boys had brought rations. There was a corn field nearby, and in order to give our artillery a better sweep at the enemy's position, a section of the fence of this field was pulled down and our gun placed in position. Our 'artillerymen' slept by their gun while the rest of us found repose on the bare ground. I slept but little that night. It was my first experience in anything like organized warfare and the excitement of the occasion banished sleep. Although we had orders to remain still and quiet, yet, at all hours of that long night the low hum of conversation was heard through the encampment. It was a clear, still evening, and the stars seemed to shine with an unusual brilliancy, but a little after midnight gulf clouds overspread the sky and by morning a dense fog settled down upon the earth. On account of this fog daylight seemed a long time in coming and before it was good light we were all in line and ready for the fray. It was then discovered that during the night the Mexicans had fallen back a short distance and taken position on a mound. While reconnoitering our scouts were fired upon and as they fell back upon our line the Mexicans, about twenty-five or thirty in number, charged toward our position. Col. Moore directed Lieut. Dickenson to open on them with his 'artillery' and this order was instantly obeyed. The shock caused by the fire of that old brass cannon seemed to jar the very earth and the sound seemed sufficient to awaken the dead. It awoke the echoes for miles around and, figuratively, it continues to reverberate around the earth as the gun that sounded the death knell of Mexican tyranny in Texas.

"At the discharge of the cannon the Mexicans wheeled and fled with all speed to their main line, while their flight was greeted with a round of cheers such as only exultant Texans could give. I don't think a man or a horse was hit by the missiles fired from the old gun but the sound was the agency that checked their course and sent them pell-mell back to a place of safety.

"A very few moments after this occurrence Capt. Castenado advanced to a point within hailing distance and asked to have a talk wtih 'el Comandante.' Col. Moore approached him and after an exchange of civilities, beckoned Capt. Coleman to come forward. At this time Castenado called to one of his men who in response joined the group. History records the conversation that took place between Col. Moore and Capt. Castenado. I did not hear it. I bear record only to what I saw on that occasion. Both armies were in full view and the intensity of impatience that pervaded our ranks was only relieved when Col. Moore and Capt. Coleman were seen to wheel their horses and dashed back at full speed toward our lines, Col. Moore shouting as he came up: 'Charge 'em, boys, and give 'em hell.' Instantly our 'artillery' belched forth a volume of flame and smoke, slugs, and sound, and with a yell that still rings through the halls of my memory, that little army of determined Anglo-Saxons rushed upon the enemy with an impetuosity that brooked no resistance. The Mexicans fired one volley, then took to their heels. We lost not a man nor was one wounded. We captured a few escopetas which the Mexicans had dropped or thrown away in their stampede, and also a few blankets, and two or three swords, besides a lot of other articles of which we stood in need. By two o'clock we were back in Gonzales, safe and without a scratch. The citizens had prepared a bounteous meal, a great feast of cornbread and barbecued beef, and a dance in the open air was kept up nearly all night amid joyous revelry and frequent hurrahs for Texas.

"As to the number of Mexicans killed in the skirmish, there have been several statements, nearly all of which vary.[1] I can only vouch for what I saw. I saw two of the soldiers lying dead within thirty feet of each other only a few yards from the hillock or mound they held when we charged them. From the number of blood stains on the ground there must have been several wounded and carried off by their comrades. A few days after the fight a squad from Fannin's company, with John Tumlinson and one or two of my company, while out a few miles from town examining a trail supposed to have been made by Indians, came upon a newly made grave, and over this grave three rude, wooden crosses. Evidently there were three bodies buried there, and they must have been Mexicans, as the grave was in line of Castenado's retreat, and besides, Indians in those days did not place crosses above graves of their dead.

"While matters were thus occurring in and about Gonzales, the spirit of war and a desire to fight spread, and events of moment were transpiring (though without concert of action) in other sections of the country.

"On the 10th the cheering news came that Capt.

---

[1] Some writers, characterizing this as the brilliant commencement of the Texan War, say that 30 or 40 of the enemy were killed or wounded.

TALL MEN WITH LONG RIFLES

Geo. M. Collingsworth, with a hastily assembled party of about fifty 'neighbors and citizens' had determined, coincidentally as it were, to march upon and capture the Mexican garrison at Goliad. On the way a thrilling incident occurred. While groping their way in the dark the party accidentally came upon a lone traveller, who proved to be no less a person than Col. Ben Milam. The old hero having recently escaped from prison in Mexico, was returning to his countrymen in Texas, and had halted by the wayside to rest. This incident is related as quite a dramatic one, and the addition to their ranks of such a brave soldier and intrepid leader gave the little band of volunteers much joy and a marked degree of boldness.

"Pushing forward, the party made a strategic night attack, and after a short but brisk engagement, took the fort, killing three and wounding seven Mexicans. The surprise was complete and the victory an easy one. With axes the door to the room where Col. Sandoval slept was hewed down and the officer made a prisoner. As the Texans rushed upon the place a sentinel hailed, and fired. A rifle ball laid him dead upon the spot. The discharge of fire arms and the tumult of human voices now became commingled. The Mexican soldiers fired from their quarters, and the blaze of their guns served as targets for the colonists riflemen. One of the colonists who spoke Spanish called upon the garrison to surrender. The Mexicans asked for terms. 'No, and I cannot hold my men back longer. Come out quick if you wish to save your lives. If you resist further my men will massacre every one of you. Decide quickly. I cannot hold my men back longer'. 'Oh! For God's sake keep them back', answered the Mexicans. 'We will come out and surrender immediately'. And they poured out and laid down their arms. Thus was

Goliad taken, and the victory was an easy one, the only casualty on the part of the Texans being the wounding of Samuel McCulloch, who received a musket ball in the right shoulder, and which he carried for fifty years. This was the first blood drawn from the Texan side in the war.

"The occasion was a happy one for Col. Milam, and when the fight was over he is reported to have said: 'I assisted Mexico in gaining her independence, I have spent more than twenty years of my life in her service. I have endured the heat and cold; hunger and thirst; I have bourne losses and suffered persecution; I have been a tenant in every prison between this place and the City of Mexico, but the events of this night have compensated me for all my losses and all my sufferings'.

"The Mexican soldiers were paroled and sent out of the country, and Capt. Phillip Demitt, a very chivalrous soldier, with a small company of volunteers, was left in charge of La Bahia.

"While the engagement at Goliad was an insignificant affair of arms, the capture of the place proved of much importance in the campaign that followed, since it broke the communication between Bexar and the Gulf, which the Mexicans were never able to restore, and one of our historians says the attempt to do so lost Santa Anna the battle of San Jacinto.

"A few weeks later, on November 5th, the wood and dirt fortifications at Lapantitlan, some twelve miles above San Patricio on the Nueces, were captured. The Comandante, Capt. Rodriguez, with a company of Mexican bandits was holding the place and robbing all traders and travellers who chanced to pass, going east or west, and it was determined to oust the thieving gang. Its capture was quietly effected by Adj. Ira Westover, a very fearless young officer who had been detailed for that purpose by

Capt. Dimmitt at Goliad.

"The 'fort', with a small company of soldiers, surrendered without firing a gun. But the main force of eighty or ninety mounted men, was out on a raid and did not return until the afternoon of the next day. The Texans kept a sharp lookout, and intercepted the band of cutthroat marauders a short distance out on the Nueces where a very spirited fight ensued, in which several of the Mexicans fell, including Captain Garcia. Finally the enemy fled leaving the Texans masters of the field.

"The fortifications at Lapantitlan were demolished and the artillery, consisting of two four pound cannon, was consigned to the channel of the Nueces river."[2]

[2] Referring to this "gallant and daring enterprise" historian John Henry Brown says: "The successful affair of Lapantitlan, on account of its advanced geographical position and the interference of its garrison in stopping intercourse with the Rio Grande, was hailed throughout the country with a joy altogether beyond its intrinsic importance." History of Texas—vol. 1, p. 375.

CHAPTER III

The Flags of War Fly as Houston Arrives

"History tells of the trend of affairs and of the movements of the colonists preceding the actual outbreak of the Texan War; of how they met in popular convention at San Felipe town in April, 1833, praying for redress of grievances and drafting a constitution for separate statehood as a member of the Mexican Federation; of how they sent Stephen F. Austin as Commissioner to the City of Mexico, begging due favors of the supreme government; and of how their beloved leader and councellor was arrested and thrown into prison where he languished for more than two long years.

"During Austin's enforced absence at the Mexican capital affairs moved slowly in the Texas colonies. But the spirit of revolt and the determination to be free did not diminish. Austin's final release and return to Texas was the spark that set the smoldering fires ablaze. Everywhere the beloved man was hailed with great delight by the colonists. The gladsome news spread from cabin to cabin and from settlement to settlement, and joy overspread the land. The noble peace-loving Austin had been convinced that war was now the only course to pursue; and he at once took his proper place as a controlling spirit in the approaching crisis.

"Austin's return to his home town was heralded as a gala event; and it was my good fortune to go with my brother and some of the neighbors to the colony capital on that occasion and hear his address to the settlers. I will always remember meeting the great impressario and I thought him one of the noblest and most striking figures of a man I had ever beheld. I was forcibly impressed with the eloquent appeal to his beloved people, urging them to diligently prepare for the defense of their homes and their liberties. He declared that he had been greatly deceived by the glowing promises of Santa Anna; that events during the past year or two had convinced him that henceforward, no reliance whatever, could be placed in the pledges of the Mexican dictator, that if Texans tamely submitted to the impositions and demands of this two-faced tyrant their vassalage would be no less galling than that so recently imposed upon the patriotic but helpless people of Zacatecas. I regret that I cannot recollect Austin's fine patriotic speech on that occasion; and it seems strange that so far as I know, our histories make no mention of this address at San Felipe. He closed by saying, 'I will wear myself out by inches, rather than submit to Santa Anna's despotic rule'.

"On our return from San Felipe, I found that the people of our section along the Guadalupe were of the same mind as those at the 'Capitol' and 'war with Mexico' was all the talk. In a few days a messenger came in post-haste calling upon all able-bodied men to go at once to the relief of the people of Gonzales, who it was reported were besieged by a strong force of Mexicans. How the settlers responded has already been told. We will return to Gonzales and the 'seat of war'.

"The war was on. Our 'Lexington' had been fought, and the ball of revolution was now in motion —to gain momentum in its onward course. Austin's return to Texas and his noble and patriotic stand seemed to have been the signal for action; the spark that set ablaze the war-spirit and caused a more united action among the Texans. The news of the first clash flew over the country as if borne on the wings of the wind. The people were now aroused to a sense of their serious situation. Meetings were held in every town and settlement from the Guadalupe to the Sabine and volunteers were being hastened forward. The slogan everywhere was 'On to San Antonio', and drive every band of armed Mexicans across the Rio Grande. These men began coming in on the 4th and continued to arrive for a week. They came in squads and small companies, armed with such weapons as each person was able to furnish. Generally, they were well mounted, but of provisions they had none other than that procurable by the slaughter of beeves, and bread from corn gathered from the field and pestled into meal.

"During this time Gonzales was the scene of much activity and preparation. Among the volunteers there was a number of men who were 'jack-of-all-trades' and their services were utilized. There were blacksmiths, saddle makers, and gunsmiths. These were the most useful men in the army at that time. A detail was sent out to burn charcoal for the forges, and every settler was called upon to bring in all the scrap-iron and implements he could spare. The response was evidence of the patriotism of the Gonzales people. Women brought in their flatirons, pots, and skillets. One lady removed the spindle of her spinning wheel and brought it in to the shop. Men brought their farming tools, hoes, plows, etc., and freely gave them to the service of their country. The common expression from these patriotic people was, 'If we whip the Mexicans we can get more tools; if the Mexicans whip us we won't need any more tools.'

"Old man Asa Sowell conducted the principal blacksmith and wood-working shop in town and it was now a very busy place. All around the shop rude workbenches were improvised for the workmen. The fires in the few forges were kept up almost day and night, while the mechanics worked unceasingly.

TALL MEN WITH LONG RIFLES

Lanceheads were turned out by the score, and when our army set out for San Antonio we had a full company of lancers. But the men soon tired of these weapons and threw them away. We had provided ammunition for our 'artillery' of course, and all the old castings obtainable were broken up and stored away to be used instead of grape and canister. Men were set to work on a gun carriage. They felled a large cottonwood tree in the river bottom, and sawed from its trunk four sections for as many wheels, these being about four inches thick and were strengthened by strips of timber nailed on transversely. When the vehicle was finished and the old cannon mounted thereon it provoked a shout of laughter among the boys, but it was our 'artillery' and we were proud of it.

"Among those patriots who labored apparently without rest, I clearly remember Noah Smithwick. He was a natural mechanic and could get more work out of the men under his supervision than any other man in the army. He was a giant in strength, a humorist, always jolly, and a general favorite among the boys. The last time I ever saw Smithwick was about the beginning of the Civil War. I understand he moved to California and spent the remainder of his life there.

"While all this preparation for an early advance was being made, the question of a flag came up. Some of our leaders wanted to march and fight under the Mexican national colors; others wanted the eagle, cactus, and snake, eliminated from the flag and in their stead a star. But it was soon ascertained that the boys wanted nothing that bore the slightest resemblance to the flag of Mexico. At a meeting of the officers a committee of five were appointed to select the design for our flag. This committee was to report by three o'clock the next day. And this gave the occasion for the loftiest display of patriotism on the part of the women of Gonzales. They knew that material for a flag was scarce. Before ten o'clock the committee in council was overwhelmed with offers of material of all shades, textures, and fashions. A few silk dresses that had doubtless been worn on state occasions 'back in the states' and were now faded and tattered—but religiously treasured as sacred mementoes of happier days—were brought forward and freely offered. One heroic mother whose sons went down in the Alamo the following March, brought her only pair of green window curtains.

"It was finally decided by the committee that it was the duty of the Consultation to design and adopt a flag of the new nation; that any action in regard thereto would be premature and not binding; but in view of the present conditions it would be right and proper for the army to have a banner under which to march during the present campaign, and that in keeping with the simplicity that characterized the general make-up of the army the said emblem be as follows: a white field without border, in the center a picture of a cannon, unmounted and without any fixtures whatever, directly over the cannon a five pointed star. Under the cannon and near the lower margin in large letters extending nearly the length of the flag, this inscription: 'COME AND TAKE IT.'

"The flag committee's report was received and its recommendations accepted, and the following day we had a flag raising, when, for the first time, the *Lone Star* was flung to the breeze. I know that to Miss Troutman, a young lady of Georgia, is conceded the honor of having designed the first *Lone Star* flag of Texas, and that a Georgia company first waved that flag at Velasco, in 1836; and while I would not deprive that girl of any honors due her sacred memory, yet I must bear witness to the fact that the 'cannon flag' designed and hoisted at Gonzales on October, 10th, 1835, was the first *Lone Star* that was ever caressed by a Texas breeze—unless that honor should be given to the Dawson company standard, made by Mrs. Dawson of Harrisburg, Texas, in September, 1835, and presented to Captain Andrew Robinson's little volunteer company, of which her husband, A. B. Dawson, was First Lieutenant. As I remember, this Dawson flag was of ordinary solid color 'calico'-tri-colored, red, white and blue, and emblazoned with a five pointed white star, set in the red background, the three color bars being set perpendicular, or upright, the red, with the star next to the flag-staff. The flag was of rather small size and was never recognized by the army as their flag, but as a company standard. It was highly prized by the Harrisburg men, and was much in evidence on the march from Gonzales to San Antonio, being borne by Second Lieutenant Jim Ferguson. I remember seeing this flag at our camp on the Cibolo, and I think it was carried on to Conception. What its fate was I do not know. I have heard it was left in the Alamo when most of the volunteers went home during the Yuletide of 1835, and that the fragments of the precious little banner were found among the ruins after the fall of the fortress, March 6th, 1836. But whether or not *this* Lone Star flag was ever hoisted by Travis and his gallant comrades to wave over the doomed fortress, will never be known. I believe that it is generally conceded that the Alamo men battled and died under the Mexican tri-colored flag of 1824—the emblem of constitutional liberty in Mexico. It would have nerved these resolute patriots in their dying hour had they known that Texas had declared its independence and was floating a flag of its own—the Lone Star. Such is the irony of fate.

"About this time, on the 10th, I think, Stephen F. Austin arrived at our camp and was given quite an ovation. All looked upon the great man as a wise councilor and a safe leader, and so he was unanimously chosen as our commander-in-chief with the title of general. To heighten the excitement and arouse further enthusiasm, at this juncture the general received a message from Colonel Cos, at Bexar, saying that he was coming to Gonzales with a large force to recover that cannon. When this news was circulated among the boys their enthusiasm was raised to the highest pitch. 'Let them come and take it', became the cry.

"All being in readiness, on the morning of October 13th, 1835, we took up the line of march for San Antonio. After crossing the Guadalupe west of town the commander and his staff took position on an eminence ahead of the column and remained there until the troops had passed in full review. Before starting, however, Captain Coleman ordered me and another lad about my age to report to the general for duty as orderlies. Fortunately for us we were near our commander on a little hill and saw the army file past with some semblance of military order. The force, now swelled to five or six hundred, was the largest body of men under arms that I had ever seen and the impression made on my mind was second only to that made by General Arista's great army in battle array at Palo Alto some ten years later. From our vantage point we could see the entire command as it crossed the river, ascended the west bank to the open valley, and marched past. I remember our cannon flag was proudly borne by a man mounted upon a small, wiry pony that had an inclination to dash off at full speed every time the boys gave vent to their feelings with a ringing cheer, which was quite frequent. Immediately following the flag and the 'color guard' came our 'artillery' under the command of Captain Almeron Dickenson, with his company of artillerymen, all of whom were mounted and wore no insignia to distinguish them from any other branch of the service. The gun carriage, as previously stated, was an ordinary four-wheel truck. And just here, while I do not wish to gainsay or discredit any of the statements made by other eye-witnesses, as at my advanced age my memory of events and incidents of those early days may be at fault, yet my recollection is that this truck was drawn by horses and not by oxen as some have contended. And this stands to reason, since there was comparatively no scarcity of horses, and owing to the slow gait of the oxen, no troop would have thought of using them as draft animals on the cavalry march when every volunteer was eager to cover the distance in the shortest space of time.

"Our artillery company headed the column on the first day until towards the evening, when the gun carriage broke down while crossing a small creek. While it was being repaired the column marched past, and from that hour the old cannon was in the rear and by its occasional breaking down became the source of more delay and vexation than any other feature of the march. We managed to patch up the frail running gear until we reached Sandy Creek and went into camp, when Captain Dickenson informed the general that in order to proceed further with the gun, a more substantial carriage would have to be provided. Before breaking camp next morning many of the boys, through curiosity if not reverence, went to 'artillery Headquarters' to look at the wreck, I being of the number. General Austin, Colonel Moore, Ben Milam, and others, were in consultation with the chief of artillery, and while some were in favor of repairing the gun carriage, and holding on to the old cannon at any costs, others, among whom was Milam, advocated its abandonment. I heard him tell Austin that unless a supply of ammunition (expected from Goliad) reached us in a very few days the gun would prove useless; that from reports from scouts, General Urgatachea would doubtless meet us with a large force on the Salado, where in the open we could whip him and capture his guns as easily and as surely as we had chased them off at Gonzales; that there were plenty of cannon at San Antonio, and that even if Urgatachea declined to meet us at Salado, all that we had to do was to go on to San Antonio and take guns and garrison. It seems that Milam's suggestion prevailed; the gun was abandoned, the army took up the line of march, and I never saw the old piece again. I was told, and it was common report among the boys in the ranks, that Captain Dickenson had the gun buried on the spot; and in order to conceal its resting place from enemy scouts who might chance that way, the ruins of the truck, with wood and brush, was piled upon the shallow grave and burned, thus leaving only a pile of ashes indicating a campfire. The question is often asked as to what became of the 'Gonzales cannon,' and I have endeavored to answer that question. Its recovery would add a priceless relic to the collection being made by the Daughters of the Republic of Texas, and I believe that I could yet locate our encampment on Sandy Creek, and the spot where the old brass gun has lain for all these years.

"We reached the Cibolo on the 16th and remained in camp a couple of days waiting for reinforcements which we had been informed were coming from East Texas. It was here that I first saw the renowned Sam Houston, and I shall never forget the incident. We had just gone into camp for the night on the bank of the Cibolo, when a lone horseman—his length of limb sadly out of proportion to that of the horse he rode—came up in our wake and was greeted by Austin as 'General Houston.'

"Though personally a stranger to the greater portion of the company, his record as a fighter was so generally known that not a few were the regrets that he was not at the head of the little army. Austin, though a favorite with the army and a man of cool and undoubted courage, did not impress the volunteers as a fighting man, and his apparent delay in pushing forward led some of the hot-headed patriots to the conclusion that Houston would be the man to hasten the campaign to a successful conclusion. Houston's fame had preceded him to Texas and he was looked upon even then as a hero. He was of magnificent form and features and looked every inch a great military man and leader.

"Most of us felt that Houston came to assume command. His visit, however, had a different motive; he came in the capacity of an envoy to secure the cooperation of the army in the scheme of absolute independence of which he was a strong advocate. We had hitherto given little thought to the political aspect of the movement, but Houston's argument, set forth in a speech he delivered to us after supper, carried with it such weight that when on the morrow he departed on his return to San Felipe to attend the convention summoned to decide the course of the colonists in the impending crisis, he carried with him the full power to speak for us in the conclave. Houston was not only brave but he was wise, and was then shrewdly laying plans for his own campaign, and his visit to the army was, no doubt, for the purpose of testing the temper of the volunteers and getting an idea of how he was held as a leader.

"His most potent argument in favor of independence was the position it would give us in the eyes of other nations. 'So long,' said he, 'as we are only contending for our rights as a province of Mexico we can claim no recognition or assistance from abroad; but let us declare for absolute independence and appeal to the liberty loving people to help sustain us in our position and help will be accorded.' He also proposed to enlist the Cherokees as allies, a measure which he, no doubt, could have handled successfully; but the United States, whose jurisdiction extended over these Indians, would not permit this breach of good faith with Mexico; though Mexico evinced no such conscientious scruples.

"Houston's ringing speech had animated and kindled the flame of patriotism among the boys to a high tension and made us all the more anxious to push on and into San Antonio.

"On the 20th, our army reached the Salado[3] and went into camp, where we remained for a week when another forward move was made, and a position selected near the old Mission Espada, about ten miles below town. But I am anticipating some interesting and thrilling incidents which occurred en route, and which I will now relate."

(3) By the Mexicans this word, "Salado," is pronounced "Sallow," accent on the last syllable with short o as in how, plow, etc.

CHAPTER IV

Famous Fighters March Upon San Antonio

"Before breaking camp on the Cibolo, and as a precautionary measure, Lieutenant Tomlinson, with a small squad of picked and well mounted men, was sent forward to reconnoiter. I was one of the number selected. We left at daylight, and had not gone far before we discovered Mexican 'signs' in abundance. When within about four miles of the Salado we came upon a plain trail which showed that a small herd of beef cattle driven by about twenty-five men had passed along only a few hours ahead. Pushing forward with considerable haste we came in sight of the foragers at the river and opened fire. The Mexicans were greatly surprised and after an exchange of shots fled in confusion. We gave hot pursuit for two or three miles, and in the running fight Henry Karnes killed one, and another was captured. The captive had his horse killed under him in the first fire at the Salado, and as his horse fell he sustained severe bruises at the knee and was unable to flee with his comrades. In the melee the Mexicans had left several horses, stampeded during the skirmish, and it was while rounding up these animals that the wounded man was discovered. In point of intelligence this fellow was above the average Mexican, and he seemed disposed to give us any information that he possessed. He told us the day and the date General Cos had reached San Antonio; the number of men he brought; and that since the arrival of the entire Mexican army —over twelve hundred strong—Cos had been working day and night strengthening the fortifications; that they had eighteen cannon, mostly large caliber, and provisions sufficient to enable the garrison to hold out against a siege until Santa Anna could come to his relief. To us it was amusing to hear this fellow relate the estimate the Mexicans in San Antonio had formed as to our strength. He said Generals Cos and Ugartachea had full and correct information as to our movements, the number of men in our army, number of cannon, etc.; and that our forces amounted to about two thousand men of all arms, including four hundred and fifty Cherokee Indians under Houston and Chief Hunter. The prisoner told his story with all seriousness, and it showed the state of feeling that prevailed in Bexar.

"And here I will relate an incident, of no historical importance, except as marking the scene of our little 'racket' on the Salado. While waiting for the command to come up Karnes detached the steel lance head which he had taken from the Mexican he had killed, and with his ax which he carried on his saddle, drove it into a small pecan tree about four feet from the ground. Several years later while in old 'Paint' Caldwell's company at the battle of Salado, I saw this lance head well imbedded in the tree, and many years later, about 1859, I saw it again, but the growth of the tree had nearly concealed the marker from view.

"The army coming up remained on the Salado until the 27th, waiting for reinforcements which were still hastening to join our ranks. Meanwhile many were clamoring to go forward, urging that we were already strong enough to take San Antonio; that while we were loitering around waiting for more men Cos would also be receiving reinforcements and would be further strengthening his fortifications.

"About this time our army received a valuable addition in the person of 'Deaf' Smith, the celebrated spy and scout, and in this way: He and his son-in-law, Arnold, had been out on an extended hunt of several weeks, searching for a rich silver mine which an old Indian whom Smith had once befriended, described as existing in the wild mountain regions skirting the Lampasas River. Smith had come to Texas at an early day, settling in San Antonio; had married a Mexican lady and became a loyal Mexican citizen. When he returned from this hunt the war had broken out, and as he attempted to enter town a squad of Cos' cavalry fired upon him and chased him out. Some of the Texan scouts, seeing the race, went to the rescue and saved Smith from capture. On account of family ties Smith did not at first wish to take sides in the row, but he was mad now and determined to cast his lot with the Texans and take revenge on the treacherous Mexicans. I well remember seeing the old scout as he rode into camp with Karnes and several others. He already had a reputation as an expert trailer and as an Indian and Mexican bandit fighter, and those who knew him extended a hearty welcome. Without dismounting he went to General Austin's tent and tendered his services, saying, with some excitement: 'When I came in yesterday and approached town, I was halted at a Mexican outpost. After explaining who I was and my desire to see my family, the officer informed me that I could not pass until he had consulted General Cos. When I went again today, and while talking to an officer, I saw a squad of cavalry galloping forward, and when the officer attempted to grab my bridle I wheeled my horse and dashed away. The dirty scamps fired upon me and came in a dead run. I gave them a parting shot and under spurs and quirt won the race. But there will be another day, and I'll get even with the treacherous rascals.'

"Deaf Smith was soon made a chief spy, and he gave a glorious account of himself. He was called 'the eyes of the army,' and was a great favorite with

Sam Houston. The only picture of the old scout is from an original portrait painted for the General by a noted artist who visited the Republic just after the close of the Texas Revolution.

"While the army lay on the Salado we were not altogether idle. Through the good offices of Ambrose Rodriguez, General Austin was kept posted on matters in Bexar. Rodriguez was a resident of the place and one of the few Mexicans who had cast their lot with the Texans, and rendered much valuable service. Evidently to impress us with his strength and daring, Cos each day sent out bodies of cavalry to approach our camp. Our scouts were always on the alert and invariably charged such forces, but only to see the cowardly cusses turn tail and break for town. On these occasions the enemy usually outnumbered us ten to one, but they never risked a fight, seemingly being endowed with a wholesome fear of the 'Filibusteros,' as they called the Texans.

"It was about this time also, on the march between the Cibolo and the Salado, that the famous Jim Bowie joined the army. Bowie was a prominent citizen of San Antonio and he had married a daughter of Vice-Governor Veramendi. But he was still a patriotic American, and when war arose he did not hesitate in casting his lot with the struggling Texans —soon to gain immortal fame.

"At the Salado quite a number of recruits came in, swelling our ranks to about seven hundred men —all clamoring for a fight. Orders were now issued to move forward, and at noon on the 27th the force went into temporary camp at Mission Espada, on the San Antonio River, and about ten miles below town. A scout of about ninety men was selected and sent out under Jim Bowie and James Fannin, to reconnoiter and select a more favorable position nearer town.

"We left about noon and reached Mission Conception late in the evening, going into camp in a bend of the San Antonio River where there was a low ground or bottom with high banks skirted with timber in front and the river in our rear. As we struck camp an old padre from the mission paid us a visit and appeared very friendly. It was suggested that he was a spy and should be detained, but Jim Bowie coming up recognized the priest as an old friend and assured the boys that the padre was a trustworthy man, and so he was allowed to go unmolested.

"Soon it was noticed that the tenants about the mission were in a state of excitement, and this gave us reason to believe that a runner had been sent to warn General Cos of our presence. Thus, forewarned, we used the utmost caution for the night. Our horses were secured in the open space of the river bend, strong guards were posted and a sentinel placed in the tower of the Mission church.[4] The night was still and clear, but before morning it became cloudy and a heavy fog rested over the valley. Before dawn the boys were up and had partaken of a repast of jerked beef and cornbread, and most of them had their horses saddled ready to mount and make an early reconnaissance of the town before the main force came up.

"I and brother Josiah had saddled our horses and breakfasted when two or three of our comrades came along and asked us to go with them to the picket line to relieve the guards for their breakfast. Josiah declined the invitation, but leaving my horse in his care, I took my gun and went along. When we reached the post on the high ground in the direction of the mission, we found Henry Karnes on

(4) Robert J. Calder was the man who kept watch from the church tower.

duty. The fog was very dense and as we came nearer, Karnes was stooping and peering through the gloom as if trying to locate some object. In a low tone he told us to listen, that he believed he heard the sound of hoofs. A few moments later we were fired upon by a large body of Mexican infantry which had silently approached under cover of the fog, and the continued blaze of their guns made a lurid scene. Returning the fire we fell back towards the river bottom. Just before we scampered down the high bank, and while yet exposed to the enemy's fire, Karnes exclaimed 'Boys, the scoundrels have shot off my powder horn.' And right here I wish to digress for the purpose of correcting a small error that has crept into history. It has been recorded that Karnes was never known to swear but once and that was when the Mexicans shattered his powder horn at Conception. I was within three feet of Karnes when this incident occurred, I heard the musket ball strike the horn, and heard distinctly his expression. He used some very strong invectives but I am quite sure he used no 'cuss words.'

"As we turned down the bluff the boys were forming all along the brow of the elevation and preparing to repulse the charge. Fannin's company occupied the ground in the lower part of the river bend, while Coleman's held the upper side. In places along our (Coleman's) front the brush was in our way and at other points the declivity was too steep for a foothold. With our hunting knives we soon cleared away the bushes and along the steep places we cut steps so that we could ascend, fire, fall back and re-load under cover.

"As the sun rose the fog lifted, revealing a force of some four or five hundred Mexicans, who now rushed up and began a furious attack, pouring a continuous fire—it was almost like a solid sheet of flame. It was my first taste of real war and it was a nerve trying experience. Captain Bowie urged the boys to be cool and deliberate and to waste no powder and balls, but to shoot to hit. And it was at this time that I first remember having seen a blue-eyed, fair-haired boy about my own age. He carried a long hunting rifle and was dressed in a buckskin hunting suit and fur cap. I noticed during the fight that this youth never fired without taking very careful aim, and every time his long gun blazed, he would duck his head and look under the smoke to see if he got his man. After the fight was over I made inquiry as to who the young marksman was, and was told that his name was Si. R. Bostick. We soon became acquainted, and from that day there sprang up a friendship between us which has lasted for nigh onto seventy years, strengthening and ripening with each recurring year. In truth, as I relate these incidents, I believe we are the only survivors of that band of heroes whose bravery and prowess in and around Bexar in the latter part of 1835, gave Texas the brightest pages of her incomparable history.[5]

"The Mexicans now brought up a brass-ribbed four-pounder and opened a rapid fire on our position with grape and cannister, which, however, passed harmlessly over our heads. This gun was being worked eighty or ninety yards from our position and the gunners became targets for the crack riflemen along that part of the line nearest the cannon. It seemed that at one volley every artilleryman hit the dust, and those who took their places shared a like fate. When they were driven back the third and last time, and while their officers were vainly trying to rally them on their colors, which had been placed on the cannon, Jim Bowie shouted,

(5) Veteran Siron R. Bostick was one of the last living survivors of the battle.

'The cannon, boys! Come on and let's take the cannon.' And with a wild cheer the men rushed forward, seized the Mexican color standard, wheeled the gun, which was loaded, and turned it on the enemy who fled in the direction of San Antonio. The fight was over.

"The Mexican loss in this affair is said to have been 60 killed. I did not count them but I saw quite a number of dead Mexicans lying around over the field, and I believe the slain far exceeded the number given by our historians. I know it was a matter of comment that day among the men that the dead far exceeded the number of wounded left on the field, which was something unusual in open battle.

"The wounded evidently expected instant death at our hands and it was indeed touching to hear their piteous pleas for mercy. I had approached a young Mexican of good appearance and above the average of intelligence. He lay where he had fallen with a broken arm and a bullet through his bowels. He held up his hand and begged me to spare him, saying that he was fatally wounded and wanted to see the padre before he died. I spoke kindly to him and assured him that Americans never killed prisoners and wounded men. He complained of great pain and begged for water which was freely given him. Others of the wounded were given water and such assistance as could be rendered, until the arrival of the old padre, our visitor of the evening before, who came to minister to the dying and to care for the dead. His duplicity had no doubt brought on the whole trouble and he must have felt remorse of conscience as he viewed the sad sight.

"Our loss was one man killed, Dick Andrews, a brave fool-hardy patriot, who actually threw his life away during the fight. We all had been cautioned to keep under cover of the embankment and the trees and not unnecessarily expose ourselves. At one time during the engagement, it became necessary for our company to rush to the assistance of Fannin's men to help repulse a stubborn charge of the enemy at that point. Instead of keeping along the bottom, which was protected by the elevation in our front, Andrews took the near way across the open space, and in full view of the Mexicans. A shower of bullets was sent after him as he dashed across the open space, and he fell mortally wounded. He lived long enough to know that we had won a victory. But, poor fellow, the ball entering at the right side, came out on the left, lacerating the bowels in its cruel course. He lingered for several hours, suffering the most agonizing torture, begging all the while to be relieved, and the poor fellow would place a finger on each of the bullet holes and try to tear them open in frantic efforts to alleviate his sufferings.

"We buried our comrade that evening beneath the spreading branches of a pecan tree and with military honors, a volley being fired over his body from the two cannon captured from the Mexicans in the fight. Jolly, big, Dick Andrews, always of happy disposition and not easy to provoke to madness, was a favorite with all, and not one of us but that shed tears as the body of our beloved comrade was laid to rest. He was a true soldier, brave as a lion, and his name will go down in history as being the first martyr in the cause of Texas liberty.' Andrews county is named for him and will perpetuate his memory to the latest generation of Texas youth.

"A man named Pen Jarvis was wounded during the action, and in a very peculiar way: a ball striking his Bowie knife in such a manner as to drive the sharp blade some depth into his body and inflicting a very painful wound, but he survived. Ever afterwards this fellow was called 'Bowie-Knife Jarvis.'

"This, and I pass to other incidents of the long ago. Nearly three score and ten years after the battle of Conception, or 'The Horseshoe,' as we called it at the time, while attending the 'Battle of Flowers' at San Antonio, in April, 1904, I went over the old battle ground. What a change the hand of time and the encroachment of man had wrought! The ground was in cultivation, the timber had disappeared, the old mission was in ruins, and 'even the river seemed less wide.' And here, perhaps, it might not be out of place to say that we fought at Conception without a flag, and without the beat of even a drum, although I have heard fledgling San Jacinto Day orators speak in spread eagle style of the 'Lone Star flag that waved in heavenly grandeur over the flame swept field of Conception.' But there was no flag or banner of any sort in our rank on that occasion; nor was there any music on either side—only the sound of cannon and the rattle of musketry was heard. Our 'Cannon Flag' had been left somewhere on the route from Gonzales to the Salado. The last I saw of it was on the morning when the cannon was abandoned at Sandy Creek. It had been furled and was resting against a sapling nearby. It may have been used as a winding sheet for the old brass gun or it may have been employed for baser purposes."

CHAPTER V

Burleson Commands as the Quasi-Siege Begins

"The brilliant victory at Conception was a telling blow, and it had its depressing effect upon the enemy, causing them to look with more alarm upon the movements of the 'diablos Tejanos.' It proved that those 'tall men with their long rifles' were more than a match for the gaily uniformed, well-drilled, and amply armed Mexican soldiers; and it certainly inspired and increased to the highest pitch the enthusiasm of the volunteers. They had started out with the slogan, 'On to San Antonio,' and it was now changed to 'Into San Antonio.'

"During the progress of the fight, and just before the fog cleared, a runner was sent out to headquarters for help, the entire force hastened forward, but arrived upon the scene just after the action was over. Had the force reached Conception an hour sooner the campaign no doubt would have ended a month earlier. The entire Mexican force would have been killed or captured and no doubt the Texans would have pushed right on into Bexar and captured the place at one fell blow. Of course most of the boys were chagrinned at having missed the chance to fight and wanted to push right on into town and 'mop up the whole greaser outfit.' So strong was their clamor that a hurried 'council of war' was held, but from some cause no marching orders were given, and the army went into camp. I know it was camp gossip that General Austin favored an immediate advance but that he was opposed by certain officers of his staff. I could name them but I would not impugn the character of any of the patriots of Texas. They all meant well, but some were misled by certain more designing and less patriotic men.

TALL MEN WITH LONG RIFLES

"The spot selected by Bowie and Fannin for our army camp was a most excellent one from a strategic point, but the boys were tired of camp life —they came to fight, not to 'flare around,' and every one was singing, 'We'll soon be in town.' Orders came to advance the whole force, and so, on the last day of October we found ourselves on what was known as the 'Acequia del Alamo,' or Alamo ditch, near the Old Mill. And right here I want to correct an impression that has long prevailed in the public mind about this 'Old Mill.' Many have been lead to conclude that this mill so often mentioned by Texas writers, was a corn mill erected and operated by the inhabitants of San Antonio. A great mistake. This old mill was used in former days for grinding cane. It was of primitive design, not unlike those crude contrivances used by the early settlers for grinding sorghum cane. This particular mill was known to the Mexicans of San Antonio as 'La Trapiche de Caña de Zambrano.'

"A day or so following our arrival at the Old Mill we were moved out to the hill north of the old 'Powder House.' At this time we had not less than one thousand men, and this number was continually augmented until the force aggregated at least twelve hundred men, all ready and anxious for action. There were two or three companies of 'Old States' volunteers, and their officers made a show towards maintaining army discipline, but the Texans generally went where they pleased and came when they chose. There was no insubordination, but there was a spirit of restlessness among the men that was difficult to control and the officers were unable to enforce anything like camp discipline. To a certain extent the men were losing confidence in their officers who had promised to lead them into battle, not to move them around from pillar to post and try to teach them how to use their rifles. Day after day the question was asked: 'When are we going into Bexar?' But when? Quien sabe!

"From our close-up position overlooking the town, we could see the troops drilling, could see them passing to and fro between the Alamo and the military plaza, and at all hours of the night we could hear the cry of their 'Centinelas Alerta.' Thus the days rolled by into weeks, and the men became more disheartened and disgusted. From captured Mexicans it was learned that General Cos was daily expecting a strong force under General Ugartachea, and yet there was no prospect of an early advance. Our officers were in daily consultation, but they never seemed to agree upon a plan of attack. The men, seeing the vacillation and uncertain state of affairs, began to leave. There was no power to restrain them, and by the first of December our army had been reduced to less than six hundred men.

"Thus passed the second month of our campaign. But from the time we reached the vicinity of San Antonio we had not been altogether idle. A quasi-siege had been maintained and several attempts made to decoy the enemy into traps outside the walls, but they were wary. Deaf Smith, Jim Sylvester, and others, had friends among the Mexicans in town and these they visited at nights. In this way we learned that owing to the scarcity of forage, General Cos planned to send his cavalry horses to pasture on the Rio Grande. A sharp watch was kept for the departure of the herd. Scouts were posted South and West of the town during the day and their numbers doubled at night. On the morning of the 14th a runner dashed into camp with the news that the herd was moving out of town under a strong escort. Captain York's and Switcher's companies, about fifty men in all, lead by Bill Travis, went in pursuit. When about five miles out, and seeing our approach, the Mexicans made a feint as if to turn the herd and fall back towards town, but as we dashed upon them the escort fled, leaving the entire *caballada* of about three hundred miserably lean, but fairly good, horses. We also captured several of the escort, their mounts being too weak to allow them to escape. The captured horses were rounded up and sent to pasture on the Colorado.

"On the 25th of November, General Austin having been appointed a commissioner to raise money and men in the United States to help carry on the war, resigned and left the command. The selection of a new commander followed. The younger element of Texans wanted Milam for their leader, but the volunteers from the 'states,' aided by the older Texans, elected Edward Burleson, with Frank Johnson as adjutant. The old Ranger chief was known as a brave and successful Indian fighter and it was thought that he would be more aggressive and lead the boys into battle at once and without 'red tape.' But no—something was wrong. About this time, however, on the 27th, I believe, occurred quite an amusing incident which served at least to break the monotony and give the boys some fun, if not reward. During the month and more that we had been encamped around Bexar the quasi-siege had been maintained, while scouting parties under Bowie, Travis, Deaf Smith, Bird Lockhart, and others, were constantly scouring the country in the direction of the Rio Grande, as far as the Nueces, watching for the enemy and burning off the grass so as to destroy nature's forage for the horses of any advancing force. Meanwhile Cos and his army were in a precarious situation, cooped up without supplies and their horses nearly starving. From deserters and prisoners it was learned that Cos was daily expecting the arrival of supplies, and funds with which to pay his troops. The report also spread through the camp that General Ugartachea was coming with a large force to Cos' relief. These stories, while perhaps groundless, only served to excite the Texans to the highest pitch. It must be borne in mind that these gallant men were fighting without pay and were ready to take any chance in attacking and appropriating the Mexican army chest. The road leading in from the direction of the Rio Grande, the route over which the treasure train would be expected to pass, was watched with vigilant and eager eyes.

"In his extremities Cos found it expedient to send out foraging parties under cover of night, to cut and bring in grass for his horses. Now it so happened that early in the morning of November 27th, I think, Deaf Smith, who had been scouting through the country west of town, dashed into camp and reported having seen the long looked-for Mexican pack train slowly approaching. Over one hundred men, with as many pack animals, had been counted. This news was hailed with a wild cheer. Visions of suddenly acquired wealth floated before each Texan's eyes. All was excitement and activity. Our commander, General Burleson, urged caution on the part of the men. He believed that this pack train and escort was only the vanguard of Ugartachea's army and it was with an effort that he prevented his entire force from taking part in the proposed capture of the advancing caravan.

"Bowie was ordered to select one hundred men to reconnoiter and give attack if he deemed it expedient. Calling Deaf Smith to his side, Bowie asked him to choose twelve of his best marksmen and boldest riders to lead the van. Henry Karnes was the first man called and was immediately followed by others until it seemed that the whole army was ready to abandon camp. All in readiness, the party set forth at rapid speed to capture the 'treasure train,' while others, without orders or leave, slipped out on foot. Meanwhile, seeing the approach under a cloud of dust, the Mexicans beat a hasty retreat towards town—the ladened and braying burros following in their wake.

"On the Alazan creek, a short distance from town, at the point where the Castroville Road now crosses, the enemy was encountered and the Texans made a furious attack. The fight was brief but sharp, and after considerable loss the 'greasers' fled helter-skelter and in great confusion, every fellow for himself to escape the fury of these 'diablos encarnados,' as they called the Texans. The coveted pack train was in our possession. But our chagrin and disgust knew no bounds when we found that instead of silver coin, the packs contained nothing more than grass which was intended for the starving horses of Cos' cavalry inside the walls of Bexar.

"This ludicrous affair, almost approaching a battle, was then dubbed and is since known in our history as the 'Grass Fight.' How many of the enemy were killed and wounded, I never knew. We Texans were more intent upon securing the treasure than in capturing the frightened 'greasers' and so let them escape with their dead and wounded comrades. Our historians vary as to their estimates of casualties. Yoakum gives the number killed at about fifty, with several wounded. Of course this estimate may be approximately correct, but I cannot believe that such a large number were slain. If true, the 'Grass Fight' should rank as one of the real battles of the war. In truth I do not believe that half that number fell in the engagement. Our only casualties in the fight were two wounded and one man missing. It was said that this man became so frightened or excited during the melee that he actually ran away on foot at breakneck speed, and never finally halted until he reached the settlements.

"Some amusing incidents happened during the scrap. One Texan was hit a glancing shot, perhaps by one of his own party, in the first charge and fell from his horse. After the excitement was over a party went to look after their fallen comrade. He was found sitting on the bank of a small ravine, holding his forehead with both hands. One of the party, John McGuffin, called out in a jocular tone, 'Hello, pard. What are you doing? Catching your brains in your hands?' The wound was painful and had somewhat dazed the man.

"Yoakum says that the 'Grass Fight' has been greatly confused with another occurrence on the 8th of the same month, which happened in this wise:

" 'A party of thirty-two men under command of Capt. William Austin, went out in search of Ugartachea. When they arrived at the place where the 'Grass Fight' afterwards occurred, one of their number, House, was accidentally killed. The party went on, sending back Lynch for another party to bring in House's body. Fifty men were accordingly dispatched for that purpose. As they were returning with the body they were attacked by 250 mounted Mexicans. The Texans took post in a gulley and continued the fight successfully, till they were reinforced from their main camp, when the enemy was driven back with a loss of fifteen or twenty killed and wounded. The Texans lost none. The accounts of the 'Grass Fight' and of the affair of the 8th are derived from statements of those engaged in them and are considered reliable.'[6]

"All of this may be true; but it is passingly

(6) History of Texas, Vol. 2, p. 19.

strange that I never knew of this engagement; never heard of such an affair being discussed by men in camp.

"And now I pass from these somewhat minor incidents to one of the most heroic episodes in the history of the military affairs of Texas."

CHAPTER VI

Who'll Go with Old Ben Milam into Bexar?

"The heroes of the Texas Revolution introduce themselves in rapid, gallant style: Colonel Moore and colleagues at Gonzales; Collingsworth and comrades at Goliad; Bowie and Fannin at Conception; Deaf Smith and others in the 'Grass Fight'; Austin and Burleson around San Antonio; and now the noble patriot and intrepid old soldier, Ben Milam, bursts upon the attention of the reader with all the impetuosity of his liberty loving nature and in most glorious manner.

"The Texan army had encamped about San Antonio for a full month, maintaining a quasi-siege, but one altogether too inactive for the restless and impetuous citizen-soldiers who were anxious to push on into town and deal the enemy a crushing blow—the victory at Conception and the few skirmishes following, only serving to whet their appetites for a real fight. Each day brought new recruits who, if possible, were more clamorous for an immediate advance upon the old Mexican town. We could hear the drums and bugles of the enemy morning and evening and our scouts approached sufficiently close to enable them to see that unusual activity was being displayed in strengthening the Alamo fortress and the main plaza defenses.

"When Burleson took command the army was divided, one faction arguing that it would be a piece of unwarranted foolhardiness to undertake to capture Bexar. Cos had an army, they contended, of one thousand or more well armed and trained troops, that the streets of the place were commanded by many heavy guns, and to undertake the reduction of the old stronghold with only two small pieces of artillery, would be an act of unexcusable madness. Those in favor of the assault brought forth the argument that, while the town was well fortified, the Mexicans could not stand up before the Texas riflemen; that their numerous big guns, as observed by our own spies, were so placed that they could not be trained other than along the streets; that in their rude embrasures they could be veered to neither right nor left, and by keeping to the houses on either side the assulting columns would be out of reach of their guns; that General Cos did not have over six hundred effective men in Bexar, and that his ammunition was short, his men on half rations, unpaid and woefully disspirited, all of which was true as was eventually shown.

"I distinctly remember the excitement that prevailed in the camp when an order was issued to raise the siege and retire to old Fort La Bahia (Goliad) for winter quarters, and I remember that the younger men, those sons of the early colonists, were loudest in their protests—demanding that they be led forward to the assault.

"Meantime, on the 2nd of December, the fiery Colonel Jack had called the men together and made them a speech, in which he declared that it would be an everlasting shame for Texans to turn their backs to the enemy and go truckling home. He said our mothers would be ashamed of us, our sisters would despise us, and our country would brand us as being a set of cowards and weaklings, unworthy to bear the name Texans. He closed his ringing speech with a call for volunteers who were willing to join in a determined attack upon the town, and perhaps four hundred men rushed into line, wildly shouting, 'On to Bexar.' 'Down with the Mexicans.' Among those who came forward were many of the volunteers from the 'States.'

"When quiet was restored, General Burleson ordered those who favored an immediate attack to fall in line, and when drawn up, he made a short speech in which he stated that at dawn the next morning the assault would be made; that we should get our arms and ammunition in good shape, since there would be some desperate fighting at close quarters and every man should be well prepared. Of course we knew nothing of the plan of attack and cared less—all we wanted was to meet the enemy.

"December 3rd dawned cloudy, dank and chilly. Long before daylight the boys were astir, expecting every moment to be ordered into line. But no orders came, nor was a satisfactory explanation ever given as to why an assault was not made at this time. The only explanation I ever heard was to the effect that one of the men who opposed the attack, had deserted during the night, and had no doubt reported our plans to Cos. Of course much excitement and rebellious feeling now prevailed. Burleson counseled the men to remain quite until further developments came, and for the boys not to think that he was going to turn his back upon the Mexicans until they had whipped him, and that could never be done so long as he had a Texan soldier left.

"And now another exciting incident occurred. About three o'clock on the following morning, three Americans, Sam Maverick, Jack Smith, and a Mr. Holmes, non-combatants, and residing in Bexar, aided by Deaf Smith, succeeded in making their way out and to our camp. These men gave a full report of conditions in town, the numerical strength of the Mexican army, the number of cannon, the scarcity of supplies, and the general discontent of the men. All the boys soon gathered at headquarters to see and hear these men, and there were several short and sharp speeches made by different individuals, some few opposing, but the greater number favoring the taking of Bexar.

"At this juncture the excitement was further increased when one of the scouts, Bates Berry, rode up with a Mexican officer whom he had captured while scouting below the 'Old Mill.' Of this villainous fellow and arrant horse-thief and of his tragic fate at a later period, the novelist, Captain Mayne Reid, has graphically told in his absorbing narrative, 'The Headless Horseman.' Lieut. Vauvis gave a report of the conditions of Cos' army which coincided with that just reported by the three Americans. An interpreter was called and as the excited men drew near to hear and see, their menacing presence gave the lieutenant extreme alarm and, mistaking me for a Mexican, he appealed to me for protection, declaring that he had deserted the Mexican army and was on his way to our camp when intercepted. I gave him assurances that soon allayed his fears.

"Naturally, these incidents and reports tended to increase the discontent and somewhat mutinous spirit of the restless and disgusted volunteers, many declaring their intention of leaving the army if the officers did not do something at once; that home would be better winter quarters when Texas was free of 'greaser' soldiers and that they would never retreat before Mexican 'escopetas.' Somehow I felt that something was going to happen and that pretty soon, and as I stalked around among the boys I told them to be patient, that I believed they would soon see some of the hottest fighting they had ever experienced.

"Thus matters stood. But as the hours passed the climax approached. Ben Milam and Frank Johnson were heard in animated conversation, and presently they were observed walking rapidly in the direction of the commander's quarters. Minutes now passed as hours. Suddenly the flap of General Burleson's tent was thrown back and a man stepped boldly out and forward. He drew a line on the ground with the stock of his rifle. Then waving his old slouch hat above his head, he cried in stentorian voice, 'Boys! who'll go with Ben Milam into Bexar?' The quick commingled responses, 'I will,' were almost deafening. 'Well, if you are going with me, get on this side,' shouted Milam. And with a rush, animated cheers, and loud hurrahs, the men formed in a line to the number of about three hundred—every one eager to follow the old hero in any venture and at all hazards.

"Burleson, who had stood the while silent, but looking on in approving manner, now stepped forward and made a stirring appeal to those who stood back. He showed that many of their comrades were going into the town; that a reserve force was needed; and that since they were unwilling to join in the assaulting column they should remain in camp and be ready to assist in case of emergency. He further told them that to abandon us at this critical moment when every man was needed and expected to do his duty, would be treasonable and would be looked upon by all Texans and by the people of the 'states' as an act of basest cowardice. 'Remain like men,' said the speaker, 'and win or lose, you will share the glory with your brave comrades. Abandon us, and you will merit the contempt of posterity!'

I well remember some of the quips of merriment on that eventful day; which showed the spirit of levity and joviality that animated the boys on the eve of the most daring achievement in all previous Texas history. One of those who had been loud in his contention to retreat, said, 'I wouldn't mind going with you fellows, but I have no gun. My horse fell with me yesterday and broke the stock of my rifle.'

TALL MEN WITH LONG RIFLES

'We'll take you along to cut bullet patchin,' roared Frank Johnson; and for years afterward that man went by the name of 'Bullet Patchin.'

"Much activity now prevailed in camp and the remainder of the evening, and until far into the night, was spent in preliminary organization, polishing guns, distributing rations and ammunition. In fact, but few of us slept any that night. The excitement was too tense. At last we were 'going into town.'

" 'Tall Men with Long Rifles' were in evidence in the camp that night, and the boys were as joyous as if waiting a festive affair. Long before dawn of the day every volunteer was ready, anxious for the fray; but as they armed, formed, and fell into line for marching, a marked decrease in the levity was observed—they all felt, and knew, that great danger confronted them, and that they must do some tall fighting to achieve victory over such a well armed and strongly fortified enemy. I afterwards talked with many of the men who joined Ben Milam and followed him into that desperate struggle. Everyone realized the seriousness of the situation and the desperate fight ahead; and yet not one of them ever doubted but that they would win victory over the fearful odds. It was valor and long rifles that won in that fight."

CHAPTER VII

Milam Meets His Death in the Texan Victory

"The first campaign in the war of Texas independence lasted about three months, closing in a blaze of glory. The capture of Bexar was one of the most brilliant affairs in our history. The mode of battle was planned by the intrepid Ben Milam, and was won by some of the tallest fighting ever done on Texas soil. The victory was a glorious one; the pity is that the heroic old soldier fell in the very hour of victory.

"The attack was to be a break-of-day surprise, and the conditions favored the plans. The beautiful starlit night had given way to heavy fog, a curtain of mist hung thick around every object, concealing forms but a few feet distant. The plan of attack was well executed. Col. Niell, with one of the guns and Capt. Roberts' company, was sent in advance, and silently crossing to the opposite side of the river, took position commanding the Alamo. Ere long the peal of Niell's cannon told he was at his post of duty, and with this signal the main force began their silent march toward the mist enshrouded town. For two hours Niell's gun played upon the fortress—more as a feint to draw the enemy's attention while the main force attack was to be directed toward the barricaded plaza.

"With the first boom of Niell's cannon the glad words, 'Forward, boys! We're going into town!' rang out and the men were in motion. The two divisions had been formed, their courses divergent. The first, and the one to which I was assigned, was led by Colonel Milam; the second by Colonel Frank Johnson. The advance of both divisions was prompt and simultaneous, Milam's marching down Acequia street and having for its main point of attack the Navarro House; while Johnson's force entering the town at the head of Soledad street, was to take the Verimendi place. Each column moved under direction of experienced guides and along its designated course in single file.

"As our advance scout under Deaf Smith approached the Verimendi place they encountered an enemy picket with whom they exchanged shots. The Mexicans now sounded a general alarm and opened fire from every quarter. Our instructions were to waste no ammunition and to hold our fire till well within range. The streets along which we approached were swept by Cos' artillery, planted in the barricades at the plaza, but we soon found the report of the spies touching the range of these guns to be true. They had been trained to sweep only the center of the streets, and a man on the sidewalk on either side was in little danger of being hit by a cannon shot.

"Our troop was here divided, one advancing from jacal to jacal, from house to house, on one side; the other following the same course on the opposite side. The advance of the two main divisions while some distance apart, were yet almost on parallel lines, and for the first two days of fighting were in reasonably close communication. The enemy's fire increased as we drew nearer the plaza where the buildings were stronger and more compact, all of them being of stone or adobe with flat roofs; and a wall projecting around and about four feet above the surface of the roof. These walls were manned by Mexican troops who kept up a brisk fire upon us during the day, and if they had been trained marksmen, armed with any other gun than the 'escopeta,' few of us would have escaped death. I saw volley after volley fired from an 'aratea' in our front and not a man's head to be seen. Crouching behind the roof-walls, those

TALL MEN WITH LONG RIFLES

Mexican soldiers would load, thrust their guns over the crest of the low wall and send a constant shower of balls in our direction, with harmless effect. On their part it was a matter of self-preservation, since no sooner did a head appear above the walls than it served as a target for a dozen hunting rifles, and there was always another dead Mexican. As night came the terrible fusilade of small guns and the deafening roar of the artillery ceased. My division had not lost a man, while the enemy had suffered heavily.

"With the lull of the guns and under cover of darkness we made considerable advance, erected a few barricades in exposed places, and at dawn of the second day pandemonium again broke loose. While we were engaged in erecting barricades during the night, the enemy had not been idle, and when the fight began that morning it seemed that Cos had assembled his entire force in front of Milam's division.

"Our historians in their accounts of the storming of Bexar, have had much to say about our artillery, and doubtless readers have often wondered why Milam and Johnson did not bring this artillery into action on the first day of battle and demolish those barricades about the plaza. The truth is we had only two old cannon—a six, and a twelve pounder, and about the only service we obtained from them was the noise they made when fired. Those two guns were the ones captured in the fight at Conception; they were of ancient vintage, small bore, and at this day and time, would hardly pass as low grade scrap-iron. Moreover, most of our ammunition for these guns had been consumed by Captain Niell while firing on the Alamo, the first morning of the attack.

"When we went into action on the morning of the 5th, each man was supposed to carry two days supply of rations, but by morning of the second day there was not a morsel in my (York's) company, and every man was ravenously hungry—fighting all the day and working hard all the night gave us a ravenous appetite. But, thanks to Quartermaster Wm. G. Cook, about nine o'clock that morning, and while the air seemed filled with flying missiles, and the smoke from the enemy's guns hung in dense clouds over the old town, he sent forward an abundant supply of nicely barbecued beef. This was issued to the men while they stood or crouched under cover of fences, walls of houses, etc., and was devoured with a relish.

"When the quartermaster found that the reserve force—those who had refused to go into the assault—had nothing to do but loaf around the camp and watch us do the fighting, he ordered out a detail to bring in cattle from the range, others to bring in wood, dig pits, build fires, slaughter beeves, and barbecue meat. It was thus during the entire siege, and no man went hungry as long as he was within reach of the quartermaster. The Captain became a favorite with the men who fought at Bexar, and he later won great distinction in camp and forum. He was a member of the ill-fated Santa Fe Expedition. He married a niece of patriot José Antonio Navarro —Navarro was a native of Corsicana, and not a Mexican, as many suppose.

"The hardest fighting of the second day was in the afternoon. From the flat roofs and barricades the Mexicans poured an incessant storm of shot upon us. They brought up two heavy guns with which they knocked to pieces the few jacales and adobe walls that sheltered us. Just opposite us was a large stonehouse, and our only hope lay in getting possession of this building, although its flat roof, and those of the building adjoining, swarmed with Mexican soldiers. And now a thrilling episode of

KARNES LEADS THE ATTACK WITH A CROWBAR

dauntless daring—

"Henry Karnes seized a heavy iron crowbar which he had found, and said, 'Boys, load your guns and be ready. I am going to break open that door, and I want you to pour a steady hot fire into those fellows on the roof and hold their attention until I can reach the door, and when I break it in I want you boys to make a clean dash for that house.' 'Yes, but the building is full of Mexicans; don't you see the muzzles of their escopetas in the windows?' asked one of the men. 'Damn the Mexicans and their escopetas. It's that house or retreat. You men do as I tell you.' And with rifle in one hand and crowbar in the other, he flew across the street, and after a few well directed blows, the door gave way, by which time our whole company was at his heels.

"As we entered, it was amusing to see the Mexicans tear out through a partition door. Several were made prisoners, but were paroled at once, as we had no men to spare for guard duty. And here I digress to say that the parolling of a Mexican soldier required a slight knowledge of the Mexican character. To administer an oath after the American usage had no effect on a Mexican. He regarded it as a form of no value and, if a prisoner, he was liable to be found next day in line of battle, ready to shoot at you again. The Mexicans were Catholics, and no oath was binding upon them unless the Roman cross figured in the proceedings. So with a charcoal snatched from an abandoned 'brasero' it took Captain York but a few minutes to make a cross for each captive on the white lime-plastered wall. The men were marched up, the right hand of each on an outlined cross, their left hands on their breasts, and the oath was administered—and they observed it.

"From this point, fighting from house to house began in earnest, and it was during this procedure that our crowbar proved an invaluable adjunct as a weapon of warfare. From room to room we slowly advanced, with armed foes in front and overhead. Every room had its heavy iron-grated windows (no glass) opening on the street or into the patio—the stairway leading to the roof being on the side leading to the patio it was difficult to dislodge those overhead. With our crowbar we would punch a hole in the intervening wall sufficiently large to admit a rifle barrel. This drilling of holes was kept up until a number of openings had been made. Through these portholes we thrust our guns and fired in such rapid order that the enemy had no chance to fire back through the same openings. Very often the enemy would set up counter drilling, but with no effective results. At one time, on the third day while both sides were pounding away on an adobe wall, the entire partition fell in on the Mexicans side. There were eighteen soldiers and a lieutenant in the room, several were borne down in the crash and some badly bruised, others were almost suffocated in the dust and rubbish. All were made prisoners and paroled in the usual manner.

"In nearly all these rooms were found women and children, meek and submissive to the decree of war; and from these we received every token of kindness; and I am glad to place on record that no Texan was known to display any rudeness towards those helpless non-combatants during the entire five days fighting in Bexar. And just here a beautiful little incident will be related. A lovely little Mexican girl had concealed her pet kid from the Mexican soldiers. When we had driven them from her mother's room, and while yet battering at the next partition wall, this little girl heard one of our men ask the mother if she could give him something to eat, as he was very hungry. The little girl hastened to bring her pet out of hiding and offered it to the hungry soldier, saying, 'acceptarlo, señor mío. Es todo lo que tenémos!' (Accept it, dear, sir; it is all we have!) In one room two of our boys lay desperately wounded. Along side of our men lay six of Cos' men. The Mexican women were as tender and as attentive to our suffering comrades as they were to their own countrymen.

"Of daring and heroic deeds occuring during the assault, a volume could be written—every man fought for himself and everyone proved himself a hero. On the third day, after we had captured the house on the north side of the plaza, the Mexicans planted a cannon to the left, just outside their main works and trained it on the building we had just taken. This gun was playing havoc with our shelter. Seeing this, a young man from Nacogdoches, by the name of Sylvester, of Captain Edward's company, made a dash for the gun, shot one of the gunners, knocked another down with his rifle, spiked the cannon, and escaped back to the lines. Cheer after cheer went up from his comrades and Ben Milam declared it the bravest deed he had ever seen or read about.

"On the night of the 8th, I and comrade Si Bostick took turns guarding a number of wounded prisoners. Among the badly wounded was a Captain Raphael Avila. I administered to his comfort in so far as I could and, finding I could speak Spanish, he became quite communicative. He told that General Cos could not possibly maintain his position longer than another day; that the army was on the verge of starvation; the men disspirited; and the supply of ammunition was very low. The soldiers had been told that Ugartachea would bring a large supply of provisions, a full treasure chest, and the men would be fed and long past due wages paid in full.

Ugartachea had come, bringing a reinforcement of 500 men, but no provisions and no money. The additional troops came ragged and hungry, and they only helped to consume the meager supply of food yet remaining. 'Tonight, or tomorrow night, at most,' said the Mexican officer, 'will witness the departure of a large force under command of one of Cos' most trusted officers—they are going to desert!'

"The Garza house, the Navarro house, the Verimendi house, the house occupied by the priest, and Zambrano row now had been taken by our forces. The Mexicans still held their barricade on the main or Military plaza and also the Alamo. The Verimendi house was considered the most important of the positions we had captured. It was in front of this house that our brave Ben Milam fell; and it was on the roof of this building that Deaf Smith and Lieut. Hall, of the New Orleans Greys, were wounded. They had ascended to the roof in order to get a better view of the enemy's position. Sharp shooters were evidently watching them, and they were fired upon and wounded, fortunately, not seriously.

"There have been many accounts written of Colonel Milam's death, scarcely any of them agreeing. Being within thirty feet of him when he fell, I believe myself competent to give a correct statement of the facts as I saw them. Milam, Johnson, Cook, Morris, Karnes, York, and other leaders had assembled at the Verimendi house to formulate plans for the final assault. Milam carried a small field glass (a present to him by General Austin). With this glass, and while standing in the front yard of the building, Milam was viewing the Mexican stronghold on the Plaza. At this moment a shot rang out and Milam fell, the ball piercing his head. I heard the shot and saw Milam fall and instantly turned to ascertain the direction from which the shot was fired.

TALL MEN WITH LONG RIFLES

There was firing going on all the time, more or less, and this particular shot would have attracted no particular notice but for its fatal and most deplorable result. One of those present in the yard called attention to the fact that at the report of the shot he saw a white puff of smoke arising from the branches of a large Cypress tree that stood on the margin of the river. At this announcement all eyes were turned in the direction of that tree, the outline of a man was seen, several rifle shots rang out and the corpse of the daring sharpshooter crashed down through the branches and rolled into the river.

"After the surrender, Colonel Sanchez told Colonel Frank Johnson and Captain Bennet, in my presence, that this sharpshooter, Felix de la Garza, was the best shot in the Mexican army, a half-brother of Almonte, and that General Cos was deeply grieved over his death.

"On the morning of the 8th, General Cos called a council of war at which it was determined to withdraw his forces from the main plaza and concentrate his entire army within the walls of the Alamo. Orders were issued to this effect and the movement was begun at three o'clock on the following morning. During the early part of the night, Colonel Condille, commander of the forces on the plaza, received notice that General Cos had been assassinated and that he, Condille, should hold his position until further orders. Early next morning, at roll call, he discovered that he was short 174 men, among whom were Captain Juan Galan; Manuel Rudecindo Barragan; Adjustant Inspector of Coahuila and Texas, Don Juan José Alguazabel; and the Captain of Lancers, Don Ignacio Rodriguez. Colonel Condille was also informed that General Cos was not dead, as reported, but was anxious to know why he refused to obey his orders of the previous evening.

"When the report of these desertions spread the utmost consternation prevailed in Cos' army, and among the Mexicans of Bexar. A rumor went forth and gained credence to the effect that these deserters had gone over to the Texans and were going to turn their guns on their former comrades. Deaf Smith was credited with having fathered this report. When the news of the desertion reached our quarters we thought of the wounded Avila's statement and we all felt assured that his prediction would soon be verified.

"When General Cos was informed of the desertion of his troops, and of the intrigue, he lost his self-control and exclaimed to Sanchez, 'By the cowardice and perfidy of those whom we believed were our true comrades, all is lost. Go, Señor, and save those valiant men who are defending the plaza. I authorize you to approach the enemy and arrange the best terms possible. Save, Sir, the decorum of our government, the honor of her arms, and the honor, lives and property, of those chiefs, officers, and troops that yet remain with me and with whom I am willing to perish![7]'

The morning of the 9th was cloudy, damp and cold. From our position on the north side of the plaza, we could plainly see there was confusion in the ranks of the enemy. We saw the Morelos battalion, commanded by Colonel Sanchez, march out of their stronghold on the opposite side of the plaza, in the direction of the Alamo, taking with them their only remaining gun, a four pound cannon. A few minutes later, three Mexican officers, accompanied

---

[7] Por la cobardia y la perfidia de muchos de los que creiamos nuestros companeros, todo se ha perdido. Vaya Ud., a salvar a los valientes que defienden la plaza, y lo autorizo a Ud., de el partido que sea dable. Salve Ud., el decore de nuestro gobierno, el honor de sus armas, y el honor, vidas, y propiedades de los jefes, officiales, y tropas que aun me acompanan y aun que perezco yo." Filisola, Guerra de Tejas, Vol. 2, page 204-205.

by a bugler, appeared in our front. They wore no arms except their swords. While yet at a safe distance, they halted, and their bugler sounded a parley. In an instant the windows and loopholes in our quarters bristled with rifles each one trained on the party. We were frontiersmen who knew how to fight, but we knew little of military etiquette and ceremony. In other words we did not understand the signal, and if someone had given the order to fire, the treaty negotiations might have been postponed for the time being, at least.

"Seeing our attitude, one of the officers produced a white handkerchief which he held aloft and by this we understood their mission. Dr. Cameron was called and in company with Frank Johnson and several others advanced to meet the group of Mexican officers who proved to be Colonel Sanchez, Lieutenant Rada and Don Ramon Musquiz. When asked as to the object of their coming, Colonel Sanchez, their spokesman, said he wished to speak to our commander-in-chief. He was informed that our commander was not present but would be on the ground by nine o'clock and if they had any message for him it would be delivered at once. Colonel Sanchez then stated that General Cos desired to save the further effusion of blood and was ready to surrender if satisfactory terms could be arranged and that he, Sanchez, and the two officers with him were empowered to meet a like number of commissioners from the Texan army to agree upon the terms of surrender, and to say to General Burleson that they awaited his pleasure.

"The message was carried to Burleson who, without delay, named Frank W. Johnson, James G. Sylvester, and Robert Morris, to serve as commissioners. Dr. John Cameron was appointed to act as interpreter for the Texans, while Miguel Arcinega, a Nacogdoches Mexican, performed that office for General Cos.

"By two o'clock, or thereabouts, on the evening of December 10, 1835, the terms of surrender were agreed upon, signed, and ratified, and the town was ours. At the outset, the demands of the Mexican commissioners were exorbitant. They wanted to be permitted to march out with flying colors. They wanted us to fire a salute in honor of their flag as they took up the line of march. They wanted to retain and remove all their artillery, government stores—everything. They wanted us to furnish provisions sufficient to supply them until they reached Laredo. They wanted their parole to terminate when they passed beyond the Rio Grande. They wanted their sick and wounded to be maintained at our charge. These and many other unreasonable demands were presented and as promptly rejected. 'We are in position to dictate terms. You are the real supplicants,' said Johnson. 'Powder is as cheap as provisions, and we have the powder. We know the conditions in your army. We are willing to deal justly with you. But we intend to see that our victory shall not be wholly barren.' This brought the Mexicans to their senses and an agreement was concluded, which, in every respect, was most liberal on the part of the Texans.

"Four days later General Cos, with the remnant of his army, took up the line of march for the Rio Grande, where two months later they were joined to Santa Anna's army of invasion, returned to Bexar, participated in the siege of the Alamo, and when that venerable fortress lay in ruins, Cos said to his men, 'The fall of Bexar has been avenged: The stain of our national honor has been erased!' Cos violated his parole and when taken at San Jacinto, should have been court-martialed and shot.

"Thus was achieved by a mere handful of brave men, through the most remarkable display of chivalric daring, a brilliant feat of arms—a great victory saddened only by the loss of its inspirer and leader, intrepid old Ben Milam.

"And thus closed the first swing of our war o. independence. The Yuletide of 1835 was a happy one in Texas.

"After the capture of Bexar I obtained a thirty-day furlough and went to my home which was then on the east bank of the Guadalupe about five miles below the present site of Cuero in DeWitt County. There was great rejoicing in that humble cabin home over my return. The scattered settlers in that region gathered in to welcome me in their midst and to hear the stories of adventure and daring achievements around San Antonio. As trophies of war, I had a fine horse, bridle of costly make, a silver mounted saddle, and a beautiful sword, all of which I had taken from one of General Cos' captains. Two fine Mexican blankets, a pair of silver spurs, several silk sashes, and a pair of silver mounted holster pistols, were also among my spoils, all of which were viewed with wonder and admiration by the neighbors.

"But the pleasures of home life, in this instance, were destined to be brief. Santa Anna with a large army had crossed the Rio Grande at Laredo and was approaching San Antonio. General Urrea with a strong force was advancing on Goliad from Matamoros. Orders came from Colonel Fannin for all troops to rendezvous at San Patricio on or before the 27th of January. I was among the first to respond to this call. At San Patricio I found about one hundred men under Dr. Grant, whose aim was the invasion of Mexico. After a few days rest I was sent as a courier with dispatches for the commanding officer at Goliad who, in turn, sent me with important messages to General Houston who was then at Refugio. From this until a short time before the fall of the Alamo, March 6th, I was kept on detached duty either as a scout or courier until the burning of Gonzales.

"On the first of March I and my brothers received orders to join Colonel Niell at Gonzales. We reported at once and found about four hundred Texans, as brave men as ever shouldered a rifle, every one of whom had a record as a Mexican or Indian fighter. Most of them had been at Conception, Bexar, and the Grass Fight, and they were in high glee over the prospect of an early opportunity for a fight with the Mexicans. Travis was hemmed up in the Alamo and, as we all believed we were to go to his relief. Those of us who, under Ben Milam, had smoked old Cos and his convict soldiers out of Bexar the previous December, *knew* that we could clean up old *Santa* and his whole outfit of cut-throat 'greasers' if given a chance. That was the only theme of conversation among the boys around the camp-fires.

"On the 3rd of March, General Houston received Travis' appeal for help at the Alamo. Fannin had been ordered to leave Goliad and join his force to ours on the Cibolo. All these facts were known to the boys in camp and we were all hopeful of a great victory over Santa Anna at Bexar. Every man wanted to push on at once to the relief of Travis. We could have reached him easily in two days—by the 5th of March at the utmost; but no, we must await dilatory orders from hesitating authorities—and so the Alamo won a place in history at the price of the best blood ever poured out upon the altar of liberty."

CHAPTER VIII

Dr. Grant and His Matamoros Expedition Starts Trouble

"The filibustering spirit was rife in America during the first half of the nineteenth century, and many adventurers and soldiers of fortune stalked across the pages of history. It was the era of frontier expansion in the United States; and it was a period of unstable conditions in Mexico—the two republics were neighbors, and the great Southwest was the breeding-ground and clearing-house of unrest. The scene of action shifted to Texas during the revolution.

"The Texan revolt and declaration of war for independence attracted much attention and brought many brave and adventurous young spirits to the scene of action from every part of the American Union and especially from the bordering southwestern states—men of physical courage, dare-devils of restless spirit, ever ready and always anxious to hazard their lives in any enterprise or expedition that offered excitement and adventure; and, perchance, gain of treasure as well as added laurels of valor.

"To descend upon the wealthy border city of Matamoros and capture and loot the place, seemed easy to accomplish and soon became the favorite theme, with many willing listeners and ready volunteers. But in the end, as the sequel shows, the attempt of this enterprise proved to be the mother of the greatest misfortunes that ever came upon the colonists of Texas.

"The wild idea first originated with Dr. James Grant, erstwhile wealthy, but aggrieved ranchero of Parras, Mexico—posing as a Texas patriot—who, without the shadow of authority, marched away from Bexar with 200 volunteers, after having despoiled the handful of men left under Colonel Niell of ammunition, blankets, medical stores, and every thing else worth taking, and proceeded to San Patricio, where he expected to be joined by Colonel Fannin, Frank Johnson, and others. This was early in January, 1836.

Dr. Grant was a Scotchman who had lived several years in Mexico and owned large properties in the Mexican republic. Just when and why he came to Texas and enlisted in the struggle for independence I am unable to say, but I was told that for the stand he took against Santa Anna in the Zacatecas affair, he was forced to fly for his life, and hence came to Texas and joined the colonial army. Grant was a shrewd schemer, an adept in the school of intrigue, and withal, a visionary. If he had any of the qualities of a fighter, they were not known to the Texans, and besides he was not popular with the officers and men.

"For two weeks after the fall of Bexar the soldiers who garrisoned the town enjoyed a season of almost utter abandon. They were mostly volunteers from the 'states'—nearly all of the Texans having gone to their homes—, and being disappointed in not having their promised rewards, they soon learned to regard the property belonging to Mexican citizens as lawful prey and so acted accordingly. Each day a detail was sent out to round up beeves and fat cows for food for the garrison, and when a Mexican appeared in town with a good horse, ownership to the animal was promptly transferred to a needy *Americano*. Reliable Mexican citizens have told me of many of the practices of the volunteers while in San Antonio, all of which were a shame and a disgrace to the American name.

"Meanwhile Dr. Grant was busy perfecting his cherished scheme—the capture of Matamoros. In glowing terms he related to the boys the possibilities of the contemplated expedition. Matamoros was an opulent city. It was the port of entry for a vast territory embracing a quarter part of Old Mexico and all of New Mexico. Merchants and mine owners from Santa Fe, Taos, El Paso del Norte, Monclova, Monterey and Chihuahua thronged this great maritime mart, while Spanish hidalgos and Mexican dons reveled in oriental splendor. Matamoros was but a few hundred miles from Bexar. The country was level; grass, game and wild cattle and horses abounded, and the march to the Rio Grande would not be difficult, but rather a journey of pleasure. With a force of five hundred men—two hundred from Bexar and three hundred Texans whom he expected to join him on the Nueces—he could defy any force the Mexican government might be able to throw behind the walls of the coveted city. He dwelt upon the present condition of the troops; their inactivity; their want of supplies; the glowing prospect for pay, and the utter inability of the provisional government to render their condition any better. The taking of Matamoros would remedy all these evils. Its wealth and treasures awaited their coming and would more than compensate for all the toil, time and expense of the present and past campaign. Moreover, Matamoros, once in the hands of the Texans, their ranks would soon be swelled by thousands of patriotic Mexicans who would hail the Americans as deliverers from the tyranny of Santa Anna, and it would only be a question of time when Tamaulipas, Nuevo Leon, Chihuahua, Coahuila, and New Mexico, would unite with Texas and form a new republic with Matamoros as its seat of government.

"These glowing representations had the desired effect. The minds of these young men from the 'states' became inflamed with a desire for conquest, military glory, and loot. They were penniless, clad in rags, and had about exhausted the resources of the scant population of Bexar. It was a long stretch from San Antonio back to the 'states' and no particular blame can be attached to the course they took. On the 30th of December, Dr. Grant left San Antonio for Goliad, accompanied by 200 of these misguided young men. Colonel Niell, a patriot and a brave soldierly gentleman who was in command at Bexar, was powerless to thwart the schemes of Dr. Grant who took all the arms, munitions, clothing, and horses, that came within his reach. The medicines, which rightly belonged to the sick and wounded in the hospital, were taken and the unfortunate sufferers left to their fate.

"While Dr. Grant was employing his art of persuasion with the men at Bexar, he was bringing all his influence upon members of the Council at Washington and succeeded in winning a majority of that body over to his view touching the Matamoros campaign. And not only a majority of the Council, but many of the most influential men of the period. Fannin, and Frank Johnson favored his plans. Houston denounced the proposed expedition, and declared that if undertaken, it would in the end, prove fatal to every interest at stake. Governor Smith appointed Houston commander-in-chief of all Texan forces. The Council commissioned Colonel Fannin to the same office and gave him authority to appoint others. Houston, finding his authority in a measure superseded by others, retired for a season. Then began a long series of misfortunes sufficient to cause every patriot to lose all hope for ultimate success. And these misfortunes—the breach between the council and the governor, the disasters at San Patricio, Refugio, Goliad, and San Antonio, may be traced and accredited directly to Dr. Grant and his wild scheme for the capture of Matamoros.

"On the 4th of January, Dr. Grant and his men reached Goliad where they remained until the 12th waiting for Colonel Frank Johnson. From Goliad they marched to San Patricio where they established a general rendezvous for all who wished to join the 'Federal Army' (as Dr. Grant styled it), for the expedition against Matamoros. But the expected recruits came in slowly, and the promised supplies for the maintenance of the army failed to arrive. The winter had been unusually severe on stock and the army found itself in great need of mounts. In the valley of the Rio Grande on the Texas side roamed vast caballadas of horses, the property of Mexican citizens in Matamoros. Grant determined to secure a sufficient number of these animals to supply his army, and to that end set out in February with forty-five picked men for the Rio Grande, Colonel Frank Johnson accompanying the expedition as second in command. They crossed the Arroyo Colorado and approached within eight or ten miles of Matamoros. They soon secured all the horses they wanted—the tactics of the Comanches being largely employed in the hasty round-up and swift retreat northward. When they had crossed the Arroyo Colorado, a furious 'norther' accompanied by rain and sleet beat down upon them, and during the night two of the men and a number of the horses died from the effects of the extreme cold. Grant reached San Patricio on the 12th of February with only about one hundred animals, having lost a large number along the route. On the 16th, with fifty well mounted men, he started on another expedition to procure horses. His operations on this raid were confined to the region several leagues above Matamoros.

"On the 31st of January, 1836, General Urrea arrived with his forces at Matamoros. Spies and emissaries informed him of the raid into the Rio Grande valley and the position and the numbers of the Texans at San Patricio. On the 17th of February, he crossed the River to the Texas side with six hundred men and one cannon. The country he traversed being a wilderness waste affording shelter for neither man nor beast the march was necessarily slow. When within twenty miles of San Patricio, General Urrea received notice that a company of Texans were in camp a few miles out of town guarding about one hundred and fifty horses which were being held for pasturage. Thirty men under Captain Pretalio were sent forward with all haste for the purpose of surprising this post. At the same time the main body under General Urrea pushed forward and at three o'clock in the morning reached the town and began the action which was of short duration and before sunrise the Mexican army was in full possession, the Texans having been taken by surprise. Eleven of the latter had been killed in the brief conflict, five were wounded, while many escaped, and quite a number remained as prisoners. One banner and a quantity of arms of every description fell into the hands of the Mexicans.[8]

"Captain Pretalio attacked the camp of horse guards about the same time Urrea's men charged into the village of San Patricio, and captured the entire caballada, killing several of the Texans, wounding and capturing others. His loss was one dragoon killed and two wounded.

"Much has been written about the death of Dr. Grant, he who offered his life upon the altar of a misguided ambition. Yoakum[9] says that he was captured by forces under General Urrea on the Agua

---

[8] "Quedando muertos once de ellos, cinco heridos, y el resto, prisioneros, quedando tambien en nuestro poder una bandera y una cantidad de armas de todas classes"—Filisola "Memorias para la guerra de Tejas."
[9] "History of Texas," Vol. 2, pp. 84-85.

Dulce, taken to San Patricio badly wounded, and three weeks later was bound to the tail and hind feet of a wild horse which was turned loose, 'leaving behind him at a short distance the mangled remains of poor Grant.'

"Our good historian Yoakum made many statements which later writers could find no one to verify I met and associated with several of those who were at San Patricio before and after its capture by Urrea and have heard their versions of the occupation of the place by the Mexicans, and the events connected therewith and I never heard the story of Dr. Grant's death as related by Yoakum until after I had enlisted in General Taylor's army at Corpus Christi. I think it was while on the march to the Rio Grande, opposite Matamoros, where Fort Brown was built later, that I heard the story told around the campfire, by one of the soldiers from the 'states.' I took occasion then, as did every Texan present, to challenge the story and to denounce it as utterly false. Colonel Frank Johnson told me that Dr. Grant was killed on the Agua Dulce creek at a point not far from the present site of Banquetta, in Nueces county, and Colonel Johnson was certainly in a position to know. The Mexican account of Grant's death seems to me, the most reasonable statement on record. It accords with Colonel Frank Johnson's account, as related to me and others shortly after the sad occurance. I quote from Filisola:[10]

"On the first day of March, General Urrea, being then in San Patricio, had notice to the effect that Dr. Grant, with a party of from forty to fifty of his chosen riflemen was returning from the Rio Bravo, and he (Urrea) determined to set out with 80 dragoons to meet and surprise him. With this purpose in view he formed an ambuscade at a point

(10) "Guerra de Texas," Vol. 2, p. 409.

called Cuates de Agua Dulce, where Dr. Grant and his party would, of necessity, have to pass. Here General Urrea divided his troops which he had brought from San Patricio into six sections. At eleven o'clock on the following morning, March 2nd, Dr. Grant passed near the ambuscades or sections commanded by Colonel Garray and General Urrea. These opened fire immediately upon the enemy, and after a vigorous resistance, they were defeated. Dr. Grant and fifty-one riflemen were killed and six prisoners were taken. All of their arms and horses were captured. On the same day General Urrea returned with his forces, to San Patricio, from whence he sent scouts in the direction of Goliad where, as he had noticed, Colonel Fannin would be found with a respectable force.'

"When General Cos surrendered his army to the Texans in December, 1835, one of the stipulations was to the effect that those of his troops who desired to abandon the Mexican service were at liberty to remain in Texas. Quite a number availed themselves of this proviso, among others being one whose right name was Jesus Cuellar. Those not familiar with the Mexican language could not give Jesus the proper pronunciation and he was known among the boys as 'Ka Soos.'

"Jesus was a rare genius. He was a shrewd man, and, intellectually far above the average Mexican. He was of a jovial turn, obliging, and a model of politeness. He had acquired some knowledge of the English language and in the course of a few months could make himself fairly well understood when discussing ordinary topics. Other Mexicans who abandoned Cos called Jesus 'Comanche,' for the reason that he had been a captive among the Indians of that tribe for several years. Jesus professed great admiration for the Texans, was a staunch Republican, and held Santa Anna in great abhorrence on account of some injury the latter had inflicted upon one of Jesus' brothers who had taken part in the resistance offered the dictator at Zacatecas. Jesus was easily won over to the side of Dr. Grant and for a time was greatly enthused over the plan for the capture of Matamoros, and when the Doctor and his followers set out for Goliad, Jesus was one of the number who lead the van.

"Rodriguez, Colonel Juan N. Seguin, and a few other influential Texas-Mexicans were avowedly opposed to Grant's Matamoros scheme and when the Doctor reached Goliad, Jesus began to change his views but remained for a short time and later returned to Goliad and joined Colonel Fannin.

"When General Urrea reached San Patricio, by some means or other, Jesus learned that his brother, Don Salvador Cuellar, was with the invading army and with the cunning peculiar to his race, he soon devised a plan for the defeat and capture of Urrea's entire army. He laid the matter before Colonel Fannin who readily saw the feasibility of the plans and cordially commended the wily Jesus for his astuteness. All the details were arranged—the utmost secrecy being observed, and Don Jesus disappeard from the Texan camp. The day following there was rejoicing at Herrera's headquarters in San Patricio and Don Salvador was overcome with delight in having once more met his brother whom he had mourned as dead.

"Don Salvador Cuellar was a member of General Urrea's staff and was held in great esteem by that official and this confidence in the brother gave Don Jesus easy access to the General's credulous ear. When asked why he deserted General Cos at Bexar, he readily replied that he did so in order that he might more effectually serve his country: 'fue con el objecto de mejor servir los intereses de mi patrio.' He had carefully noted the condition of the Texan army and also gave their strength, knew the spirit that animated the people, and also gave a greatly exaggerated account of the forces then en route from the east to join Fannin at Goliad. He further stated that Fannin with 500 men was at the moment marching to attack Urrea at San Patricio, that on that very night they would march to a point within a league of the place and attack the town at early dawn. He knew the route the Texans would travel and if the General would put his columns in motion just at dark he would pilot them to a point in the dense chaparral where Fannin's men were sure to pass and General Urrea could form an ambuscade from which the Texans, taken unawares, could be completely annihilated.

"Having the utmost confidence in Don Salvador, brother of the scheming Don Jesus, General Urrea called him aside and took council as to the reliability of the new-comer and, receiving every assurance of his honor and fidelity, the General decided to pursue the course outlined by the Texano-Mexican, and immediately set out with 200 infantry, 150 cavalry, and one four pound cannon. Don Jesus took the lead as pilot and when about fifteen miles out from San Patricio, he lead them into a pass hemmed in on each side with dense chaparral and there he disappeared. Suspecting treachery when his guide could not be found and finding himself in a trap, General Urrea ordered a retreat and it was said among old Texans who passed through those perilous times that he went back to San Patricio much faster than he came out.

"Two hundred of Fannin's men lay in wait but the darkness of the night and the lack of a clear knowledge of the country caused Don Jesus to lead the Mexican force at least two miles south of the point of ambush as agreed upon and designated before leaving Fannin at Goliad.[11]

"Don Jesus remained with Fannin until Urrea's army reached Refugio and was the third messenger sent by Colonel Fannin in an effort to reach Colonel Ward at Refugio, and reached him as he was crossing the San Antonio river on the morning of the 19th. Ward, having been forced back from Refugio, and finding himself cut off from Goliad by Urrea's cavalry, was endeavoring to make his way to Victoria. Jesus showed his pluck in the action on the 20th, when Ward was attacked by four or five hundred of the enemy, but the lack of ammunition forced him to fall back in the river bottom. That night Don Jesus deserted Ward and made his way to Victoria and from that point he hastened to join Houston on the Brazos. He gave as his reason for leaving Ward, that the men were without ammunition, and that by remaining together, capture was inevitable, and so stated to Ward, advising him at the same time that by adopting the tactics of the Comanches when closely hemmed in, and scattering out, every man for himself, some would have a chance to escape, while if they remained together all would be taken. Ward gave no heed to his advice, so he decided to take his chances and quietly, in the darkness, left and was lucky enough to get away.

"When he reached Houston's little army, he joined his old friend, Captain Juan N. Seguin, and at San Jacinto fought with dauntless courage. He claimed to have fired the shot, during the charge, that killed the brave General Castrillon. When Santa Anna was brought in a prisoner, Don Jesus was one of the most clamorous for the captive's blood. The day following the capture he pleaded with General

(11) Filisola makes mention of this affair in his "Guerra de Tejas."

Houston for permission to talk with Santa Anna and when the latter was asked if an interview would be agreeable, he slowly repeated the words, 'Cuellar! Cuellar! Jesus Cuellar! No I do not wish to talk to him.' Evidently the fallen tyrant remembered the name, the bare mention of which forcibly recalled some of the bloody atrocities he had committed at Zacatecas. Don Jesus remained a loyal citizen of Texas and died at Goliad in 1841."

CHAPTER IX

An Expedition Without A Parallel In American Warfare.

To the patriots and soldiers of the Texas Revolution—those dauntless men who fought so heroicly for their freedom and independence—there goes renown and glory enough for all the future ages, without the least detraction from the real facts. When the truths of history are distorted history passes into fable.

Our historians discuss the issues leading up to the Texan War of Independence, and most of them give satisfactory accounts of the part played by the Texans in their struggle, yet little or nothing is said of the Mexican army of invasion, except as observed and encountered on the field of battle, and hence few Texans of the present generation have any great store of information regarding the organization and equipment, also the personnel, of the forces led by Santa Anna into and against the rebellious province; the difficulties to be encountered and overcome; the hardships and suffering they endured while marching from San Luis Potosi, the point at which the army assembled and from which the expedition set out. It is to add to this small store of knowledge that I offer this chapter, scraps of details gathered from various sources, largely from Mexican authorities; all of which I deem authentic because of agreement and corroboration, and which once woven into the web of the narrative, may throw some light upon that phase of history which has heretofore remained in doubt and obscurity. This record I shall offer in rebuttal to the oft-repeated statement that Santa Anna, entering Texas and marching leisurely and in pompous style—leaving a trail marked by the blood of Texan victims encountered en route—appeared before San Antonio at the head of six or eight thousand veteran troops, "the flower of Mexican manhood and valor, well armed, well clad and fed, and with a full military chest," and in this I accept General Filisola as authority, he being Santa Anna's second in command and the historian of the expedition, and withal one of the most unbiased and circumspect writers of that stirring period of whom I have any knowledge. To translate and present this Mexican historian's full account of the organization of the army and its march into and across Texas would fill a volume of several hundred pages, I will give only a brief outline of Santa Anna's movements which will be sufficient to give the reader a fairly correct idea of the men and equipment of this so-called "Great Mexican Army."

Following the revolt in Texas, Secretary of War, General Tornel, ordered General Santa Anna, as Commander-in-chief, to repair to San Luis Potosi and to proceed at once in the organization of an army for the invasion of Texas and the subjugation of the rebellious American colonists. This was in November, 1835, and during the first week in December, Santa Anna reached the designated army concentration point where he found three regiments assembled under command of General Ramirez y Sesma. These three regiments composed the first Army Division and numbered 1500 men—unarmed, poorly clad, and not a single man fit for duty! The government had placed $84,000.00 at the disposal of Santa Anna for the purchase of arms, clothing and commissary supplies for the army, and with this pittance he set about to raise, organize, and equip an amy of 6000 men with which to traverse in mid-winter a desert waste of 400 leagues in order to reach Bexar and subdue what the government conceived to be a rebellious province.

Allow me to digress long enough to say that, although President of Mexico, Santa Anna did not, and under the then existing laws, could not exercise all the functions and prerogatives pertaining to that office while in the field at the head of his army. During his absence in that capacity he was subject to the home government and received orders from the Secretary of War and was held to strict accountability for their execution. Hence, all of these statements to the effect that Santa Anna, being a dictator, was in all respects the government of Mexico, are nothing more or less than fiction.

When Santa Anna established his headquarters at San Luis Potosi, he found obstacles in his path that would have appalled any but the most courageous and determined. He immediately called upon the governors of the different Mexican states for men, money and arms. Congress had authorized an appropriation of $500,000 the previous November for the prosecution of the war against Texas, but the treasury was empty.

Through the agency of Santa Anna a loan of $400,000 was negotiated with a Matamoros firm, Señor Rubio & Co., $200,000 cash and $200,000 in supplies. With this contribution, supplemented by $100,000 out of his own private means, Santa Anna organized and equipped his army of 6000 men—after a fashion.

With all of these obstacles to meet and overcome, Santa Anna was ready to take up the line of march on the 9th of January, 1836, his forces consisting of the following:

		Artillery	
Artillerymen	182		
Zapadores (Sappers)	185		
Infantry	4473	12 Caliber	2
Cavalry	1024	8 "	4
Presidiales (Cav.)	95	6 "	4
Presidiales a pie	60	4 "	7
		Howitzer, 7 inch Guns	4
Total	6019		21 guns

To haul these guns and the general equipment, rations, stores, and ammunition, of this army, 800 mules had been secured by purchase and 1000 by impressment. Of wheeled vehicles there were 833 four-wheeled wagons drawn by mules and horses and 200 two-wheeled carts drawn by oxen. In addition to these there were a great number of carts and animals belonging to speculators and settlers who accompanied the expedition with a large supply of confections, liquors, tobacco, and other wares.

In the entire army there was not a tent except those provided by the officers for their own private convenience. Rivers and swollen streams had to be crossed, and yet one smal cart perhaps could have carried all the tools necessary for the construction of a raft or small bridge. It was in midwinter and the soldiers were clad in thin pantaloons, cotton shirts and thin jackets, and instead of shoes most of them wore "guaraches," sandals made of raw-hide.

"In all the army," continues Filisola, "there was not a chaplain to comfort the afflicted and dying; there was not a gunsmith, and only two or three surgeons and not one of these was with the expedition when the army reached the Rio Grande; they having been detained in improvised hospitals that marked every town along the route from San Luis to Laredo. To complete our misfortunes, the commander-in-chief admitted a North American quack doctor at Saltillo, through force of necessity. He was the only physician in General Sesma's division and he died of a fever on the Frio. The army was wholly without hospital stores, appliances, and general equipment for the preservation of health and efficiency, and the commissary was little better." And this is the flower of the Mexican army, "well fed, well clothed, and perfect in equipment," of which poets, orators, and writers have had so much to say!

Let us notice some of the difficulties and the hardships encountered by the soldiers and officers of this expedition. The difficulties that presented, says the historian, for the transportation of supplies were without parallel and increased day by day. "Arrieros" deserted in great numbers and their places had to be supplied. Boxes in which to ship army bread were not to be had, a box holding a quintal (100 lbs.) cost twelve dollars; there was no lumber in the country, and even if lumber had been plentiful, there were no men in the army who could make it up into boxes! The march from Monclova to Bexar was one long series of suffering and misfortune. Up to the 12th of February the winter had not been severe, but on the 13th came one of the greatest snow-storms that region had ever experienced. The day dawned cloudy and extremely cold and towards night snow began to fall, and in a few hours the ground was covered to a depth of over 16 inches (Media vara.) The cavalry under General Antsrada, while trying to reach the camping place and shelter of Ajuntas, was overtaken by this fierce storm and many of the men and animals perished during the night. The snow obliterated every trace of the road and fell in flakes as large as the palm of one's hand. The command reached an extensive mesquital (mesquite forest) where the column became broken and confused; the darkness added to the confusion, voices of command were heard on all sides, but all discipline was at an end and the men and animals wandered in all directions. The packmules were abandoned to wander away in the thorn-brush, while the drivers, huddled in groups, sought shelter from the biting cold by drawing their thin blankets tightly about their benumbed bodies, finally falling into that sleep that knows no waking. The divisions under Generals Sesma, Gaona, and others endured like sufferings, and losses of mules and oxen were heavy. The army marched in separate divisions, and each command suffered disasters, and it was several days before these divisions were reorganized and restored to order before the line of march could be resumed. It must be remembered that most of these soldiers were impressed into service, poor, ignorant Indians (a full blood Mexican is nothing more than an Indian), they were poorly paid, thinly clad and with scant rations, they had nothing to gain in this war, and desertions were numerous. The country between San Luis Potosi and the Rio Grande was sparsely populated, the inhabitants were poor and, for mutual protection against Comanches and Apaches, dwelt in towns, hamlets, and villages, and in order to obtain supplies for the army, requisitions were made on the alcaldes of these struggling settlements for horses, mules, beeves, and corn, and when these requisitions were not complied with, details of troops were sent out to gather in everything that chanced to fall within their grasp. In payment, an order on the government was issued and this was worth no more than the paper on which it was written. At San Buenaventura, Sardinas, Naradores, and Quatro Cienegas, supplies of provisions had been collected for the army, and also large numbers of horses, mules, and cattle. The Indians swooped down upon these places, destroyed that which they could not carry away, killed a large number of inhabitants, and drove off all the live stock. A detail of fifty picked cavalry under Captain Cordova was sent in pursuit but failed to overtake the savages. From Laredo, at which point the troops were encamped and prepared for the invasion, the march to Bexar was at that time a vast waste with no settlements along the route. At that season the grass was dry and water was to be had only at points long distances apart. The country abounded with wild game but this fled at the approach of the army. All that vast region was infested by savage Indians, and notwithstanding that the utmost vigilance was maintained bands of these hostiles on divers occasions hung upon rear and flank of the army, killed and scalped stragglers, and at night stampeded and drove off large numbers of horses and mules. The sufferings of the troops while crossing this stretch of wilderness between Laredo and Bexar were beyond the power of portrayal. From the Río Grande to the Medina the army left in its wake along the entire distance the wreck of carts, the carcasses of animals, and every camping place had its cemetery with graves marked with small wooden crosses. To add to the misfortunes of the army diseases known as "mal de lengua" and "telele" carried off large numbers of horses and mules.[12]

One of the most burdensome evils of the Mexican army was the large number of women and children that accompanied each division. Their presence was recognized by the authorities as an evil, but a necessary evil. Nearly every man had his "mujer,"

(12) Filisola's "Guerra de Tejas."

his woman, and many of these carried babes in their arms, and in their train were children of various ages and sexes. These had to be fed, and they shared the small pittances doled out as rations to the soldiers. Of the 1500 of these camp followers—women and children—who left Laredo with the army less than three hundred reached Bexar. They died of hunger, thirst, and exposure by the wayside. At Monclova, General Filisola and General Sesma addressed a written protest to the authorities against the presence of these women, and in reply were told that while the evil was recognized as a menace to the success of the expedition, yet it was absolutely necessary in order to prevent desertions; that without these women half the men would run away and the army would be reduced to a mere handful of men.

The wage of the common soldier was 12½ cents a day, and out of this wretched stipend he had to pay for his daily ration—the government issued no free rations—and hence may be seen the starvation allowance for the soldier after his "mujer" had shared his meager fare.

On the 22nd of February, 1836, Santa Anna, with his depleted force, reached Bexar, after a march covering a period of two months and thirteen days, enduring hardships without parallel in the annals of North American warfare.

Having taken this hasty view of the Mexican army of invasion, as it marches in divided and defiant columns across the country upon Goliad, Refugio, and San Antonio; the while the little forces of Texans scattered at the extreme outposts along the western front, doomed to swift destruction, is time to notice the most momentous and important events in the civil affairs of Texas—the Declaration of Independence. That bold stroke occurred at

Washington-on-the-Brazos on the second day of March, 1836; and in the darkest hours of Texas History.

CHAPTER X

The Fathers of Texas in August Assembly

The first gestures of the Texas Revolution closed with the brilliant affair at San Antonio late in December, 1835. The second swing of the war ended in a blaze of glory at San Jacinto, April 21, 1836. But between these two glorious events came the darkest and the most uncertain period in all Texas history.

The civil government established by the warring Texans in November, 1835, was a mistake, a farce, and a failure; and it came near blasting the hopes of Texas for freedom. Perhaps the wisest measure adopted by that quarreling crowd was the calling of a convention to assemble at Washington, on the Brazos, March 1, 1836.

That assembly is known in Texas history as the Constitutional Convention, and was the most important political gathering ever held on Texas soil, and the results of its acts and declarations were the most momentuous and far-reaching to be found in all Texas history. That course for absolute independence, had already been publically advocated by Dr. Anson Jones and a few of his bold and patriotic colleagues, at Columbia the previous December. An election for delegates to this convention had been held on February 1st, and it was universally understood that absolute independence should be declared, and vindicated by the valor of Texas arms. There were fifty-eight members in the body, comprising almost every man then prominent in Texas and many who afterwards became so. Of these individually it would be interesting to speak. Their names are enscrolled on the most precious document in the archives of Texas. Richard Ellis, of Red River, was made president of the body, and H. S. Kimball, late of Tennessee, secretary. Next day, on March 2, the Declaration of Independence was adopted. It was reported by a committee of five, composed of George Campbell Childress, Collin McKinney, Edward Conrad, James Gaines, and Bailey Hardeman, and Mr. Childress, the chairman, is given credit for its production—"he wrote it, phrased it, and penned it with his own pen, without assistance"[13] Thus was written and adopted one of the only two Declarations of Independence ever penned on American soil that were followed by successful revolutions.

The author of our Texas Declaration of Independence was one of the outstanding men of early Texas, and a dominant member of the Convention. He was a Tennessean, born in Nashville, January 8, 1804. His parents were prominent in the early history of Tennessee; his mother being a niece of the celebrated James Robertson, the founder of Nashville.

Through the influence of his uncle, Major Sterling C. Robertson, the empressario, Childress came to Texas in 1832, locating at Nashville on the Brazos. "He was a brilliant lawyer and orator, a man of great magnetism, and profoundly versed in political science."[14] These qualities and his record as a patriot and as an ardent advocate for independence commended him to the convention as the proper person to head the committee to draft the Declaration.

After the adjournment of the convention, President Burnet, appointed him as a commissioner to Washington City, to present the claims of Texas to President Jackson for recognition as an independent republic. Childress and Jackson were warm personal friends. Later he returned to Nashville,

(13) Barker's Reading in Texas History, p. 238.
(14) Fulmore's History and Geography of Texas, p. 106.

Texas, and entered the practice of law.

Like a number of other brilliant Texans of that era—Collingsworth, Grayson, Rusk, Anson Jones, and others—Childress died by his own hand. He was boarding at a Mrs. Crittendon's and early one morning in 1840, presented himself at the door before the lady was up, begging her, in piteous terms, to save him from himself. Just as she opened the door, he plunged the fatal dagger into his own heart, the blood bespattering her dress. A letter in his room stated that pecuniary losses of his brother in gaming, had prompted the fatal deed.[15]

Of all the members of the convention, not excepting Sam Houston, Childress appears to have been the dominating and most active. When news was received, and a move was made to adjourn and hasten to the scene of action, Childress vigorously opposed and prevented such a rash act. Incidentally, it may be mentioned here that it was Childress who proposed in this convention that "no person shall ever be imprisoned for debt, on any pretence whatever." Another motion of his was that "a single star of five points, either of gold or silver, be adopted as the peculiar emblem of this republic," that "every officer and soldier of the army and members of this convention and all friends of Texas be requested to wear it on their hats or bosoms."

Another very notable member of that historic convention was Richard Ellis, who presided over the body. He was one of the leading men of early Texas, having come to the province in 1825. He was a Virginian, and educated for the law. He was born in 1781, and in 1813 he located in Alabama, where he practiced his profession with much success. He came to Texas with a large number of slaves, settling near Red River in what is now Bowie county,

---
(15) Thrall's History of Texas, p. 526.

and engaged in planting on a large scale.

When Mr. Ellis was elected to the Constitutional Convention of Texas in 1836, some doubt arose as to which government the Red River section belonged to, and to be certain of representation at the proper place, a son who lived in the same house with Mr. Ellis, represented the same district in the Arkansas Legislature.

We celebrate the natal day of Texas Independence with patriotic pride. But how few know even the name of the noble patriot who presided over that fateful and historic convention which assembled at the town of Washington-on-the-Brazos in March 1836! The immortal declaration of Texas Independence which these resolute men proclaimed to the world and the Constitution they promulgated to guide the new born Republic, are models of patriotic conception, and they bristle with individualism. The assembly represented the leading men of that day in Texas, and the president of that body ranked with the ablest. Unfortunately, the fame of this noble patriot has suffered at the hands of our historians; and even the great state whose destinies he helped to shape, has shown base ingratitude to his memory. He died in 1846—the eventful year in which the Republic of Texas he had helped to make, passed away—and for the long intervening years his last resting place has been unknown to our people and it is not revealed in any history. Through patriotic promptings, his grave was finally located by the Hon. Robert Lee Henry, who wrote the following memorandum:

"Today, (March 31, 1916) I stood at the grave of Richard Ellis. He rests on an elevation about five miles north of New Boston, Texas, in the family burying ground on the old Ellis estate, established by him. Five miles further northward the Red River, with majestic sweep, courses to the Mississippi and on to the sea. At his tomb huge red oaks and giant hickories, with ample branches, stand guard over his mortal remains. At his head rises a wild plum tree with its early leaves quivering in the breezes of springtime and its fragrant blossoms exhale their perfume in this quiet and historic forest. On the strong marble headstone, toppled to the earth, beneath the image of the Lone Star, is the simple inscription:

*In Memory of Richard Ellis.
Born February 14, 1781.
Died December 20, 1846.*

He was President of the Convention that framed the Constitution of the Republic of Texas."

For one thing the members of that Convention were fearless men. The village of Washington is only about 140 miles from San Antonio. From that post Santa Anna was sending out scouts to spy on the movements of the Texans. Had he learned of this gathering on the Brazos, he could have sent a cavalry force in haste and perhaps captured the whole body. It is of note, however, that Major Williamson in command of the first Ranger force ever mentioned in Texas history, was stationed at the "Falls" of the Brazos near Washington, probably for the purpose of protecting the convention, though history is silent on this point.[16]

In the roll call of delegates to the convention it is noted that three members—Martin Parmer, Stephen W. Blount, and Edwin O. LeGrand—were from San Augustine. LeGrand was a man of more than ordinary parts; he traded in lands and accumulated a large fortune. Parmer was the most unique mem-

(16) Ford's "Old Affairs and Old Men." Ms. 4 pages.

ber of the assembly, and he took an active part in the proceedings. Blount was then and for many years thereafter, one of the prominent men of Texas. The story is told that Col. Blount had become very much angered and out with General Houston over a certain political issue. On one occasion the general made a great speech at San Augustine. Blount stood on the outer edge of the throng of listeners. As the old statesman progressed the colonel kept moving a little closer up and finally to the edge of the stand, vociferating: "Go it, my general! Give it to them!"

It is of special note that three patriotic Mexicans sat in that notable convention. Jose A. Navarro, Lorenzo de Zavala, and Francisco Ruiz. There were a number of notable Mexicans who fought with and helped the Americans in their struggle for liberty. Don Erasmo Seguin was one of the most noted and influential friends the people of Texas had in San Antonio. His son, Juan N. Seguin was in command of a company of Mexicans at the battle of San Jacinto and fought gallantly. As mayor of San Antonio he claims to have gathered up and buried the remains of the Alamo men after Santa Anna had attempted to burn them. Seguin said he buried them within the limits of the old San Fernando church. The cause which induced Colonel Seguin to leave Texas later is said to have been that his word was disputed by an American alderman. At the aldermanic meeting Seguin announced that Colonel Vasquez was on his way to San Antonio with a considerable Mexican force. The alderman said he "lied." Seguin was highly offended and left Texas. But we digress—the subject is gripping. It would indeed be interesting to make further remarks of members of that notable gathering of extraordinary men. But even a roll call and the briefest mention of each member would swell the narrative far beyond the proportion of a single chapter. The subject should attract some capable historian.

The scenes presented in that convention, and the picturesque men comprising that august body, should furnish the gifted artist with subject for a great historical painting; and such a picture would inspire patriotism in the breast of every loyal Texan. It was long the ambition of the writer to commission the painting of this great historical scene—the title to be "The Birth of Texas." To that purpose he obtained an account of the framing of our first constitution from an eyewitness, the late W. P. Zuber, who sat as a spectator in the convention hall at Washington town during most of the proceedings. The untimely death of the gifted and patriotic Texas artist, McArdle, lost such a painting to the world. Such a picture would have been a great attraction. A graphic pen picture of that notable scene, however, is left to us. Veteran Zuber wrote:

"Our Declaration of Independence is the most important event in all Texas history, and the men who composed that memorable convention and carried out its purpose, are entitled to lasting remembrance. I have always had much pride in the fact that I witnessed the assembly in session and observed the manner in which some of its affairs were transacted. The scene remains indelibly stamped on my memory. Some of the members were indeed notable and well worthy of notice.

"I saw Mr. Childress only once. That was in the convention chamber, at Washington-on-the-Brazos, March 10, 1836. He was standing by his seat (a chair) at the east side of the table around which the other delegates were seated—the chairman at the south end, and the secretary nearest him on his left. The table (built like a carpenter's work table) was, I think, about forty feet long, four feet wide, and as high as a dining table; and made of rough plank — the face or top only being dressed. There was just space enough around the table for the delegates to sit without being crowded. The dress of the delegates was not uniform, nor nearly so—some wearing Kentucky jeans, some buckskin, others brown linen, and a few broadcloth. They were nearly all clean shaven, according to the custom of that day; a few wearing side-whiskers, but none wearing mustache or goatee. Mr. Childress stood considerably nearer the chairman than the other end of the table, facing the chairman; and was reading some part of the Constitution section by section; and the other delegates voting on each by 'ayes' and 'no's,' and without debate. I stood about six feet from the southeast corner of the table, to the right of the chairman, observing the proceedings. My attention was especially attracted to Mr. Childress, as he was the only one reading aloud and the only one standing erect. Those who stood by the paper on the table, and discussed it in an undertone, were leaning over it; and even the delegate who delivered a short speech leaned over the table with his left hand on it, while his right arm vibrated gently up and down.

"Mr. Childress, standing in his boots, was, I judge, about five feet, eleven inches high (possibly six feet); straight as a shingle and well proportioned, neither slender nor corpulent. Weight, I judge, between 160 and 180 pounds. His forehead was high and moderately broad, with brow, nose, mouth, and chin, duly proportioned to it. Hair, brown or black. His face was clean shaven. His complexion was fair. I know that it was neither tanned, florid, nor pale; I term it *healthy white*. From his position, I did not observe the color of his eyes; considering his hair and complexion I judge that they were brown. His dress was in fine tastè; coat and pants, black broadcloth; vest, black silk, the cut of all being the fashion of his time,. extended considerably below the skirt of his coat, a frock coat extending considerably below the hips; shirt, white linen, pleated (not ruffled). His cravat, according to the then current fashion, was a regular black silk handkerchief, folded so as to form a band about one inch broad and fastened in front by a tidy knot, with the ends hanging from four to six inches below the throat; and the collar of the shirt was turned down over the cravat. His boots were black kid or calf, highly polished. From his appearance I judged him to be about thirty years old; though from circumstances he must have been older.

"While reading, Mr. Childress inclined his head forward towards the paper that he read; but when requested to explain the other paper, which had attracted the attention of the delegates, he assumed a perfectly errect posture, turned towards the cluster of delegates who were examining it, explained it clearly in a very few words, stood at the same spot while another delegate delivered a short speech, and till it was again voted upon; and then turned again, walked back to his position and resumed his reading.

"His posture and his step were stately, but not ostentatious; his conversation—the little I heard of it—was plain, precise, chaste, and respectful; and his voice, while reading, was loud enough—but *only* loud enough—to be heard distinctly by every person in the house, and quite pleasant. To me his size and form seemed to be those of a physically perfect man, and his manner that of an intellectual and cultured gentleman. He was in every way prepossessing.[17]"

[17] "Making Texas a Republic," W. P. Zuber to J. T. DeShields, Manuscript 4 pages written in 1900.

TALL MEN WITH LONG RIFLES

Very wisely the convention made no attempt to discuss or to settle the difficulties of the provisional government, allowing that pitiful farce to pass into history. A new and more stable government was organized, provisions were made for enforced military service, liberal land bounties were offered to the soldiers entering the army, and an appeal was issued to the people of the United States for aid. General Sam Houston was elected Commander-in-Chief of all the forces then in the field or to be enlisted, and he at once left the convention for the front.

CHAPTER XI

The Great Runaway Scrape

The high tide of success in the Texas war came to the invading Mexican army during the month of March, 1836. Meantime the cause of the Texans sank to a correspondingly low ebb, gloom overspread the land and panic seized the people. The triumphant advance of Santa Anna's great army, annihilating every opposition in its path, the siege and fall of the Alamo, the slaughter of Fannin's army, and the retreat of the little Texan force from Gonzales eastward, spread consternation throughout the country and aroused the settlers into a wild frenzy. Fear seized almost everyone, wild stories spread fast, growing in alarming proportions as they traveled, resulting in a helter-skelter skeedadle known in our history as the "Runaway Scrape."

"A true account of this colorful episode, including all of its pathetic incidents," says Creed Taylor, "has never been written and I suppose now will never be given to the world. What I shall tell may add some interest to the story of this memorable stampede.

"To understand the magnitude of the intense alarm and unparalleled panic that seized the people in March, 1836, one should note the causes leading up to the great exodus. It will be remembered that in that day we had no telegraph lines to flash the news over the country, no railroad trains, and comparatively few newspapers. All intelligence was carried by private conveyance, from lip to ear, from settlement to settlement; and like all reports of an alarming or sensational nature, they grew as they traveled until 'the three small black specks became three black crows,' and the report of Santa Anna's ruthless march was not lacking in side embellishments of Mexican inhumanity.

"That the public mind was wrought up to the utmost intensity will be readily inferred when we reflect that the proud dictator had threatened to drive every American out of Texas, to shoot every one found with arms in their hands, to destroy all their property; and when he had made his coffee with water from the Sabine, return in triumph to his capitol. San Antonio had been occupied, the Alamo had fallen, and its heroic defenders put to the sword. Then had followed Refugio, San Patricio, Goliad, and the horrible butchery of the noble and brave men who had dared to oppose the tyrant's advance. These calamities drew the pall of mourning over every home in the land, since I might truthfully say there was scarcely a family west of the Brazos which did not lose a member in one of these tragic affairs. With heroic fortitude the people bore their misfortunes, buoyed with the hope that the handful of volunteers at Gonzales—"the little ray of hope for Texas," would make a determined stand and in some way halt and crush the arrogant dictator at one fell blow—they had faith in these 'tall men with long rifles.' With this cherished hope those noble pioneer mothers and children waited and prayed for the return of their husbands, fathers, sons, and brothers. But sad, dark days soon came—all seemed lost; and then ensued that helter-skelter skeedadle—the 'Sabine Shoot.'

"My mother told me that for several days, men in small squads passed our house on the Guadalupe, almost every hour, pushing on to Gonzales. Then on a day there was a lull and the tide turned. As these men passed to the front they would stop for water and food, exchanging friendly gossip, but as they returned they were greatly excited, halting only long enough to shout, 'The Mexicans are coming.' 'Houston is making for the Trinity, the Sabine! Flee for your lives.' Then came the terrible news of the Alamo slaughter; the report was current that Gonzales was taken, all men, women and children slaughtered, and the town burned. Of course such sudden and appalling news created great excitement; the first law of nature, self preservation, was uppermost in the minds of the settlers; and thus the great exodus began.

"Soldiers often desert the army, but ours was a case of the army deserting the soldier. We may have been unduly excited, I know we were much chagrined when we arrived at our deserted army camp and saw the wild scenes of destruction about us. Under such exciting conditions, brother and I decided to hasten home to take mother and the children to a place of safety. We had caught the spirit of the occasion, and by the time we got home we had a full case of 'runaway fever.' Here we found the entire neighborhood in the throes of a great panic, a courier sent out by General Houston had dashed through the settlements along the Guadalupe, the Navidad, and the Lavaca, warning the people to get out of the country with all possible haste.

"I will not attempt other than my own experience, with the observations of a few neighbors and comrades in this stampede. Many incidents, some tragic, some serio-comic, and which would make highly interesting reading, have through the lapse of years, almost faded from my memory.

"We reached home about sundown and found mother hastily preparing to begin her flight that very night. Some of the neighbor women were there and they were all making haste to get away. Our presence gave much cheer, but it did not dispell the sad look depicted in every face. Just one little incident here will illustrate the state of feeling that prevailed at that juncture. Mother had prepared supper and while at the table just at dark, the discharge of guns not far away, was heard. 'The Mexicans are on us,' the younger women shouted, and their alarm for a while was extreme. Later in the night it was learned that some of the men who lived below us on the river, and who were coming home from the army to save their families, had fired their guns merely to announce their arrival—it certainly created much alarm.

"It should be borne in mind that one of the chief causes of the difficulties and hardships experienced by the settlers in this flight was that the exodus was begun in the early spring, a season when the range stock are in a weakened condition—no one in that section in that day provided feed for their stock through the winter. Horses on the open range were plentiful, but not having regained their flesh and strength on the tender spring grass, they were in no condition for the hard, heavy and constant trudge.

"The only wheeled vehicle on our place was a cart, with solid wheels sawed from a large log. This cart mother had decided to use in the journey. We had several yoke of oxen on the range, but they too, like the horses, were in poor shape for such a trip. However, mother had two yoke of the best and gentlest steers that she owned driven up, corralled, and ready to be yoked at any moment for the start. On this cart she planned to place a small supply of bedding, a pot and skillet or two, and some provisions. Horses for the children to ride were staked near the house.

"It is said that panics, like the measles, are catching, and I must confess that after reaching home that evening and hearing so much about the danger that threatened us, I too became possessed with a burning desire to 'make tracks in haste.' We explained to mother that if we depended on these slow oxen we could not hope to outrun the Mexican army, and that we might as well stay where we were and take our chances. 'Boys,' replied mother, 'we've got to start tonight, and we've got to use those oxen, or walk.' We finally prevailed upon her to wait until morning, when we would go out on the range and drive in the best horses we could find—for a more rapid get away. By daylight we were out on the range, and by noon we had corralled a bunch of our best horses. In the meantime and with feverish hast, mother and the children had been preparing the packs for the journey. Finally all was ready for the sad trip.

"It was about three o'clock in the afternoon when we bid good-bye to the old home, never expecting to see the dear spot again. It was not a palatial house, the furniture was scant and rude; there was no organ or piano, but few pictures and books, no carpets, but it was *home* in every sense to us, it was humble but very dear, and the children cried all evening and that night till sleep finally came to their tired bodies. If mother shed a tear I never knew it though there was an unusual huskiness in her voice that day. Mother was brave and resolute, and I heard her say to a lady while crossing the Brazos, under great difficulties, that she was going to teach her boys never to let up on the Mexicans until they got full revenge for all this trouble.

"When we left the old home we barely took time to close the doors. There was a little corn left in the crib, a large supply of nicely cured bacon in the smokehouse, and the yard was full of chickens, turkeys, geese and ducks, besides a good stock of hogs. All of these we left to the invaders. We had rigged up four pack horses, besides each member of the family carried all he or she could on their mounts. A few miles from home we overtook two families from the upper settlement on the Guadalupe. They had an ox team and were making slow progress. They persuaded us to travel with them for mutual protection. That night we camped on the edge of a dense post-oak woods, and mother insisted upon taking her turn keeping watch.

"From the Lavaca, which we crossed a few miles below the present town of Hallattsville, to the Brazos and even beyond, we were not out of sight of refugees. The country east of the Brazos was flat and low and, in many places, owing to the heavy rains, was covered with water, and here the real trouble began. People were trudging along in every kind of conveyance, some on foot carrying heavy packs. I saw every kind of conveyance ever used in that region, except a wheel-barrow, but hand barrows, sleds, carts, wagons, some drawn by oxen, horses, and burros. Old men, frail women, and little children, all trudging along. And though I have passed through the fields of carnage from Palo Alto to Buena Vista, I have never witnessed such scenes of distress and human suffering. True there was no clash of arms, no slaughter of men and horses, as on the field of battle, but here the suffering was confined to decrepit old men, frail women, and little children.

"Of course there were hundreds of incidents, tragic and otherwise, occurring in the course of the wild scamper over the almost trackless and rain-soaked prairies, and in crossing swollen streams. Delicate women trudged along-side their pack horses, carts, or sleds, from day to day until their shoes were literally worn out, then continued the journey with bare feet, lacerated and bleeding at almost every step. Their clothes were scant, and with no means of shelter from the frequent drenching rains and bitter winds, they traveled on through the long days in wet and bedraggled apparel, finding even at night little relief from their suffering, since the wet earth and angry sky offered no relief. Despite all this exposure to the elements, not one of our family suffered from sickness.

"And just here I want to record that more and greater humanity in its most exalted nature was displayed by these unfortunate people, one toward another, than I have ever witnessed. There were no strangers or aliens encountered along this terrible journey. All were friends, comrades and countrymen, with that fellow feeling which endeared a feeling of wondrous kindness one towards another.

"A touching instance is cited. The mothers of Texas have loved to tell of how a widow with four little children whose father had perished in the Alamo, was among the refugees, and that just after crossing the Colorado, the unfortunate woman became a mother for the fifth time. A family having a rickety open wagon drawn by two lean ponies, gave the helpless mother bed and transportation by throwing part of their belongings from the wagon to make room for a woman they had never seen before; and how during rains, by day or night, willing hands held blankets over the mother and babe to protect them from the downpours and chilling storms.

"Another incident I witnessed on this journey is recalled. A Texas mother whose husband was with the army, had strapped a feather bed upon her pony, fastened her oldest child on top, the next two on either end of the bed, and with her little babe in her arms, trudged along barefooted and at times so exhausted that she would sink down almost unable to rise and proceed. All through that fatiguing journey through mud, slush, and places of tall dead prairie grass, old men, frail women, and little children, walked and suffered, but no one rode alone whose horse was able to carry double, sometimes three persons.

"It was no uncommon sight to see women and children without shoes, and otherwise thinly clad, wading in mud and chilling water almost to their knees. When a cart or wagon became mired—which was an hourly occurrence east of the Brazos—there was no dearth of helping hands. But in proportion the men were few, and so the women and children were forced to perform most of the labor. Thus these half clad, mud besmeared, fugitives, looking like veritable savages, trudged along. If there was sickness, tender hands were extended, and no morsel of food was withheld from the hungry. I heard of a few deaths during the flight, but did not witness any of these sad departures. I can say, however, without any question of doubt, that they had Christian burial in so far as circumstances would admit.

"And here I will relate an incident that goes to show the bravery of those Texas mothers. The story was told to me by an eyewitness, Capt. J. H. Greenwood, who held a quasi command at Fort Houston to watch the movements of the Indians during the war. When the great runaway set in, the captain conducted quite a party of settlers from that vicinity towards the Sabine. While the party was halting on the Angelina, a body of armed men rode up and camped. They were volunteers from Tennessee led by Captain Crockett, a nephew of Davy Crockett, en route to the Alamo. News traveled slow and they had not heard of the fall of the fortress. Among the refugees were a Mrs. Moss and her invalid husband making the flight in an ox-drawn wagon. The volunteers were in need of transportation facilities, and decided to impress Moss' fine yoke of oxen, whereupon the brave woman appeared upon the scene and raising her pistol said: 'I will kill the first man that attempts to take my oxen.' One of the men made a step forward, when the plucky woman leveled her pistol and said, 'take another step and you die;' and she meant it. Captain Crockett waved his men back and rode away.

"While these refugees were again halting near San Augustine, they were startled by a terrific cannonade in the town. The mystery was explained when some men came by at full speed, shouting at the top of their voices, 'Hurrah for Texas, Houston has taken Santa Anna and his army prisoners.' This made every man a hero and every woman an angel. 'People wept for joy and embraced each other. While many prayers of thanksgiving were offered up.'[18]

"In after years it was my good fortune to know and to neighbor with some of the refugees in the 'Runaway Scrape,' and I can testify that better and nobler men and women never lived. They were a type of pioneer fathers and mothers of Texas who have passed forever with that troubled time.

"Soon after crossing the Brazos, we learned that General Houston had changed his course and was marching up the river. Anxious to know the progress of affairs in the field; and realizing that every man was needed to help combat the invaders, I decided to leave mother and the children with some friends in a secluded section of what is now Grimes county, and to rejoin the army. Several other families, feeling a degree of safety, also halted in this vicinity. But the greater number of refugees pushed on; many never halting until they reached the Sabine and crossed over to the Louisiana side. Lieutenant Hitchcock, with General Gaines at Camp Sabine, reported that the temporary camp of fugitives from

[18] Mrs. A. D. Gentry, in "Frontier Times," Vol. 4, No. 6 p. 12.

Texas, made of sheets and quilts spread from tree to tree, extended up and down the east bank of the Sabine for twenty miles, presenting a picturesque but painful spectacle.[19]

"Securing fresh horses which were had for the asking, we set out to overtake the Texan army. En route we fell in with Captain Tomlinson and a few other settlers and we all pushed forward with much haste.

"When we reached the smoking debris of Harrisburg—which had just been burned by the Mexicans —we learned the whereabouts of Houston's forces, and the close proximity of the Mexican army to the Texan camp. Our horses were becoming greatly jaded, but we could not brook the thought of being too late for a fight with the 'greasers,' so we pushed on with all possible speed. In the afternoon of April 20th, when within a few miles of 'the seat of war,' we heard heavy artillery firing and were quite sure the fight was on.

"It chagrined us deeply to think that we were not in the fracas. Spurring forward in a gallop, we reached the Texan camp near sundown, and were overjoyed to meet our comrades and to learn that we still had prospects of engaging the enemy in a real battle at any moment. General Sherman's men had just come out of a skirmish with the Mexican cavalry, and were entertaining groups of eager listeners with accounts of what they had seen and done while out reconnoitering. The general opinion was that a real fight was brewing—inevitable.

"It was on this occasion that I first met two young men who have each left their names emblazoned large upon the glamorous pages of our history—Mirabeau B. Lamar and Walter P. Lane. Lamar was a handsome, dashing little fellow, who

(19) Wharton's "Texas" Vol. 1, p. 279.

had recently come to Texas from Georgia, for the express purpose of helping the struggling Texans in their fight for independence. I remember how he was dressed, in a style different from the other boys, wearing wide-legged breeches, and a beautiful spotted-hair skin vest.

"In the hurry-scurry attack upon the enemy that afternoon, Lane became separated from his comrades and was suddenly surrounded by three or four Mexican lancers and was in imminent danger of being run through, when Lamar, seeing the situation, dashed up, knocked over one Mexican, shot another, and disarmed a third one, and thus rescued his comrade from his perilous predicament. The incident made Lamar a near hero; and as our cavalry leader in the great fight the following afternoon, he did become a real hero, winning his spurs as a gallant and fearless soldier. He became one of the leading men of Texas and was the second President of the Republic. He was one of the most picturesque and notable figures in Texas history.

"Lane goes down in history as the 'hero of three wars'—the Texas Revolution, the Mexican War, and the Civil War—and his title to fame was well earned. With Jack Hayes' famous ranger troop in Mexico, he participated in many thrilling and heroic exploits. It was he who with a few daring comrades, secured the remains of the *decimated* Mier men who lost in the 'black bean' lottery at hacienda Salado, and were lined up and shot, carrying the bones in sacks back to Texas for burial. As a Confederate general in the Civil War, Lane won great renown as a gallant leader.

"Over and above all, perhaps Lane's greatest claim to fame was as an Indian fighter. He was called the 'Fighting Irishman' and he had many thrilling exploits and desperate engagements as a

Ranger chief on the Texas frontier. On one ocasion, some two years after the battle of San Jacinto, with a small party of 'land locaters' out on the frontier, Lane was engaged in a desperate fight with a large band of Indian warriors; and which came near being his last fight on earth. It always made the Indians furious to see white men surveying their hunting grounds. This affair is known as the 'Surveyors' Fight,' one of the most desperate and bloody episodes in our border history. When all but three of the party of twenty-two men had been slain, Lane, with a badly shattered leg, managed to crawl out of range of the terrible fusilade, and assisted by his two comrades, made his way by night to safety and finally to the settlements. A monument in what is now Navarro county, marks the location and perpetuates the names of the heroic little band of men who perished in this terrible battle.

"Like myself, General Lane is one of the few old timers yet in the land of the living; and I hope to meet him and talk over old Texas days before we pass over to another Borderland.[20]"

(20) General Lane died January 28, 1892, and is buried at Marshall, Texas.

CHAPTER XII

"By the Eternal We Are Going to Win, or Die!"

Military history records many "retreats," usually of armies routed by superior forces in battle. General Houston's retreat from Gonzales to San Jacinto was not the result of defeat in battle, but rather a strategic maneuver that resulted in foiling and defeating the enemy. The retrograde movement—some call it a runaway—of the little Texan force may not be classed as one of the great events of history—the reader should remember we write of the day of small things in Texas—but the episode is historic, and the resulting consequences were of world importance.

The story told of Houston's retreat from Gonzales to San Jacinto is usually overdrawn, carrying more of censure for the commander than of unbiased facts—characterizing the movement as nothing more than a *stampede*, one that has no parallel in all the annals of Texas history—and even charging him with cowardice on that and other occasions. But for all this, no one can justly challenge Sam Houston's courage and patriotism, nor his courage on the firing line.

General Houston arrived at Gonzales on March 11—five days after the fall of the Alamo—and at once assumed command of the Volunteers, less than four hundred men, at that place. An insignificant force indeed; but it was "the little ray of hope for Texas." These raw troops were at once organized and a more rigid military discipline attempted. Rumors having reached the camp that the Alamo had fallen, on the 13th Deaf Smith, Henry Karnes, and Bob Handy were sent out on a scout towards San

TALL MEN WITH LONG RIFLES

Antonio with instructions to find out the true state of affairs. Some twenty miles out they met Mrs. Dickenson with her babe, Travis' negro Ben, and Bowie's negro servant. A Mexican messenger sent out by Santa Anna also accompanied the party of refugees, with a flag, bearing a message to the Texan Commander telling of the complete victory at the Alamo; and offering the Texans peace and a general amnesty, if they would lay down their arms and submit to his government. General Houston's reply was, "True Sir, you have succeeded in killing some of our bravest men, but the Texans are not yet conquered."[21]

Before the return of the scouts with the startling news from San Antonio, Creed Taylor with his brother Josiah and two or three other men had been sent out to reconnoiter and report about midnight. "The night (says Creed) was very dark, and as we groped our way toward camp our attention was suddenly attracted by a flare of lights in the direction of Gonzales, tall spires of flame shooting up now and then far above the horizon and illuminating the landscape in every direction. Hastening forward we soon arrived upon the scene and learned the cause of the phenomenon.

"Imagine, if you can, our utter bewilderment at finding the town in flames and our army camp deserted, with not a soldier in sight, save a few scouts who, like us, had not been called in from their posts of duty. The terrible story of the Alamo fight told by Mrs. Dickenson had caused great excitement and the army and the citizens had literally stampeded. From army comrades I afterwards learned of the wild scenes that ensued, and of how the retreat began.

" 'As the news spread,' said comrade Kuykendall,

[21] Parker's, "The Texan War," in Trip to the West and Texas, 2nd edition, 1836, p. 363.

'the alarm grew and every one seemed bent on getting away. Every fellow seemed to be for himself—it was a case of 'hoot hog, or die.' Without spiking, the cannon were rolled into the river where a short time afterwards they were fished out by the Mexicans. Most of our baggage and provisions, except what we were able to pack ourselves, was thrown into camp fires. Tents, clothing, coffee, meal and bacon were alike consigned to the flames, and all scouts and spies out on duty left without warning.'

"Among the citizens of Gonzales the excitement and distress were extreme. Over thirty of the noble men of that town had fallen in the Alamo, and the screams, wailings and lamentations of the mothers, wives, children and sisters of these brave men who gave their lives for Texas liberty and whose charred remains at the Alamo attested the wrath of the bloodthirsty enemy, will sing in my ears as long as my memory liveth, and the preacher tells me that memory, being an attribute of the soul, can never die.

"And now in the moment of this terrible sorrow came the exciting news that the ruthless foe was close upon them and they were unprepared to flee. These helpless and discomfited people must not be left to their fate. To facilitate their flight General Houston caused most of our baggage wagons to be given up to them, but the teams were yet out on the range and the intensely dark night had already set in. It was indeed a wild night of great excitement and confusion.

"Some have remarked that our Commander was unduly excited on this occasion, but I observed the General several times that evening and night, and he appeared and acted as a cool and collected man, although he exhibited much anxiety, and at times became irritated because of his difficulty in controlling the troops, also in allaying, as far as possible, the high excitement of the citizens.

"About ten o'clock one of the captains marched his company to Houston's tent and said, 'General, my company is ready to march.' The General, in a voice loud enough to be heard throughout camp, replied, 'In the name of God, sir, don't be in haste; wait until we are well ready and let us retreat in good order.'

About eleven o'clock it was announced that all was in readiness. We were now formed four deep and at the command, 'Forward, March,' we were out on our retreat—not at a double-quick gait or a hilter-skelter run, as some writers have said; and for one reason: The night was very sultry and intensely dark —pitch black—and we groped our way along quietly and in good order, making our first halt on Peach Creek, some ten miles east of Gonzales at daybreak. Soon after we set off, a lurid glare overspread the scene—Gonzales was on fire. The torch had been applied to almost every building, some said by order of Houston, but he always denied giving such orders; and I, personally, do not believe the General knew anything about the affair. At the time it was current rumor that the conflagration was started by an excited citizen when a sudden report came that a large troop of Mexicans was approaching."

"Thus General Houston, with his 'little ray of hope for Texas' began his campaign. The 'Lone Star' was shining through clouds, dimly and with uncertain luster.

"The circumstances at this juncture account for the hurried flight, both of the army and civilians. Houston was simply powerless to cope with the situation. True, he found himself at the head of a brave, but unruly and undisciplined, little body of determined volunteers at Gonzales, and nearly every hour before breaking camp witnessed the arrival of new recruits. They had heard of the appeal of Travis and were responding to the call. They came mostly in small squads of from two or three to as many as twenty or more. But they were without arms, save their sheath-knives and hunting rifles, without tents, without a commissary, without proper clothing, and without organization. And still worse, a few of the clan-like companies partook of the spirit of disorder amounting almost to mutiny and dissolution. The Alamo had fallen. 'Santa Anna, with a mighty army of ten thousand Mexicans, was approaching.' Such were the exaggerated rumors that flew from lip to ear. His spies had already reached town. They came under the pretext of bringing timely warning, but in reality as *spies*, and were now held as such under strong guard at army headquarters. 'Ere the close of another day the mounted cohorts of Santa Anna would be upon them, showing quarter to neither age nor sex. They were five hundred to one, and it was the height of folly to remain and be butchered as were our comrades in the Alamo.

"Such were the wild rumors, such the reasoning among the men. As the troops were ready to move, a man was heard to say, 'Boys, we can't leave those women and children to the mercy of the Mexicans. We ought to stay and fight it out.' Several voices spoke at once, saying, 'We have women and children of our own to protect.'

"General Houston understood the situation—he was a born leader of men. He recognized the helplessness of making a stand at or anywhere near

Gonzales, and his only object, his only hope, was to hold these excited men together while falling back, and while doing so to form them into some semblance of a real army. He went among the men, talked, reasoned, and harangued them in groups and companies, explained the situation, denounced idle rumors, and appealed to their patriotism. He pointed out the necessity of retreat to the Colorado, the Brazos, on beyond, if need be. He explained that Fannin, with 400 men, and a fine park of artillery, had been ordered to evacuate that outpost and join the regular army, and with this addition of men and arms, augmented with constant recruits from the settlements, and from the states, his army would be increased to such proportions as to enable him to meet and defeat any force Santa Anna could bring into the field; that there could be no question as to the ultimate triumph of Texas—if they only remained firm in duty and loyalty to authority. The butchery of the Alamo men, he said, would fill the hearts of all Texans with fiery indignation; the people of the United States would take up the cry for vengeance, and the call to arms would resound in every hamlet and village, volunteers would rush forward to the seat of war, and Texas would be free. Such, in substance, was the General's appeal to the insubordinate factions in his command.

"Houston was undoubtedly the best equipped and ablest man from a military standpoint in Texas at the time. But he had many enemies, and for years these busied themselves in all manner of adverse criticism. But notwithstanding all this, the impartial, unbiased historian must concede the fact that to handle this situation, to conduct this retreat, and to reach Harrisburg with a force of 700 men, required a man endowed with the highest qualities of generalship. To my certain knowledge there were less than four hundred men in the ranks when the retreat began, many of them without proper arms, and as to provisions, there were not enough carried to last two days, and these were hauled on the only two ox wagons that could be had. That was indeed a sorry plight.

"Two days and nights of marching brought the retreating forces to the Navidad, from which point the Commander wrote the Military Committee a statement of conditions, among other items of weight, saying that only twenty men had deserted the ranks. Perhaps the General withheld the actual facts for a purpose. But I have undisputed knowledge that more than one squad left on the morning of the 14th, and during the day there were more than fifty men who openly declared their intention of going to the relief of their threatened families, defying the authority of the Commander or anyone else and daring the officers to make any attempt to prevent their going —and they went. While in camp on the Navidad, these so-called deserters were reported to Houston, and he gave instructions to have every man arrested who attempted to leave the camp without permission, intimating that the severest penalty would be inflicted on those found guilty of desertion. But his orders bearing on this point became a jest around the camp fires and on the march. Desertions increased, and when the Brazos was reached there were few men in the ranks, whose homes were west of the Colorado and whose families were in the path of the advancing forces of Santa Anna; and but for the almost daily arrival of recruits from East Texas and elsewhere, the army would have been small indeed when it reached Groce's on the Brazos.

TALL MEN WITH LONG RIFLES

"The army reached Burnham's Crossing on the Colorado, near the present town of Columbus, on the 17th, crossing to the east bank of the river on the 19th, and pitched camp a few miles down stream at Beason's Mills, where they remained until the 26th of March. At that juncture Generals Sesma and Woll with a force of about seven hundred men had also arrived, pitching camp on the west side of the river, some two miles above Beason's. Houston had already dispatched an *escort* to the mouth of the Brazos for promised artillery; and every movement indicates that he expected to attack the enemy in this vicinity. But untoward circumstances upset his plans.

"General Houston has been bitterly censured for not attacking and destroying the advance columns of the Mexican army of invasion at this time and place. But most of this blame originated with his enemies, mostly men who were at a safe distance, and who lost no opportunity to undermine his influence with the people and encompass his downfall.

"There is ample proof that the Texan commander planned to fall upon the enemy at the Colorado. But late in the evening of the 25th, word had come that Fannin and his entire force had surrendered, and this startling news threw the army into a state of excitement and confusion that amounted almost to open mutiny. Men whose families were in East Texas and beyond the Brazos, remained firm and loyal, but those who resided west of that stream, and who had thus far remained in the retreating ranks, now openly avowed their determination to abandon an army that offered no protection to the settlements on the Colorado and the Brazos—and they went in such numbers that Houston was forced to abandon his plans, and to continue his retreat. That the attack would have been made and the forces under Sesma destroyed, there could be no question had these men remained loyal, and I believe that I am justified in saying further, that if all, or even two-thirds of the able-bodied men at the time living west of the Brazos, had heeded the call of their country and rallied around Houston at the Colorado, the Mexican army would never have crossed the Brazos.

"It should be borne in mind that there were hundreds of men, mostly young fellows—adventurers we might call them—who had come from the states, and who had found shelter and temporary homes among the settlers. They had no families and could easily have joined Houston, thereby enabling him to repel the advance of the enemy, but instead, they sought their own safety by flight. It was a daily occurrence for scouts and river guards to encounter carts and wagons with horses and sometimes cattle, with only one small family accompanied by from two to half dozen well armed men, all fleeing from Santa Anna.[22] Unfortunately there was no authority for the arrest of these cowardly fugitives, there was no law by which they could be forced into the ranks and made to fight the invaders, but I am glad to say—and I speak as an eyewitness of more than one occasion—these 'skeedadlers' received the treatment their disloyalty merited. Ferry guards and scouts had orders to impress all the horses, arms and ammunition, found in the possession of these skulkers unincumbered with families, and small favor was shown them. Men with families were respected— often aided—and were allowed to retain their arms and a number of horses, but those without families and whose excuse was that they were along to guard

---

[22] Relating her experiences in the "Runaway Scrape" Mrs. Rose Kleberg says, "Deserters were constantly passing us on foot and on horseback. The old men who were with families laughed at them and called to them, "Run! Run! Run. Santa Anna is behind you." **Texas History Quarterly**, Vol. 1, page 301.

the other fellow's family, were disarmed, dismounted and, in many instances, set afoot on the water soaked prairie, and left to shift for themselves. They were regarded as having no rights that a patriot should respect, and, in many instances, their personal belongings, such as blankets, clothing, etc., were appropriated 'for the good of the service.'

"The fate of Fannin at Goliad had a very important bearing upon Houston's campaign. The next day following the depressing news, Houston resumed his retreat. Before setting forth the General reported to Collingsworth, Chairman of the Military Committee, touching his decision to continue the retreat. 'I consulted none. I held no council of war.' His enemies attempted to explain this by asserting that during his entire stay at Burnam's he was on a protracted drunk—too drunk to hold a council of any kind. And just here an episode that does not make pleasant reading: For eight days the army had encamped at Burnam's on the Colorado. It had reached that point over six hundred strong and despite all desertions, according to some whose veracity I have never had reason to question, there were 1400 men in line when the march began on the morning of the 28th.

"During the eight days stay on the Colorado, General Houston made his headquarters at Burnam's house. Jesse Burnam was one of the 'original three hundred' Austin colonists and one of the early and valuable pioneers. Texas never knew a more devoted, a purer patriot, than old Jesse Burnam. He had struggled and triumphed over hardships of the wilderness and had prospered. He was in good circumstances when the army reached his place. He resided in a comfortable home which was thrown open to Houston, who occupied the best room in the house. His barns were filled with corn and hay, and these were placed at the service of the army. His smokehouse was packed with bacon and lard, and his herds of cattle and horses ranged over the prairies. All these were tendered the men, and when the army set forth for the Brazos, Burnam was a poor man. And not content with the depletion of his larder and granaries, the torch was applied, and Burnam's home, his barns and every outbuilding, were reduced to ashes. Of course Houston's enemies said the order came from Houston while yet on his big drunk. Captain Burnam, his two sons, Waddie T., and Gid Burnam, added the weight of their testimony, and I have often heard them repeat it by saying that Houston *was* drunk. The General denied the responsibility involved in the burning of Burnam's home. He alleged that it was the work of the rear guard, which acted without orders. He also denied giving orders for the burning of San Felipe, but Captain Mosley Baker went far toward establishing the fact that Houston did give him positive orders to burn that town.

"From the Colorado the Texan army marched in a direct line to San Felipe on the Brazos, and at which point every man thought a stand would be made. The men were not heavily burdened with a baggage train, since they had but little baggage to haul. They were without tents, many were without blankets, and when it rained, which was almost daily, their sufferings were intense and their march was slow and difficult. But for that strange power exercised by Houston over his men, there would have been serious mutiny, probably a fatal disruption of the army, when it reached San Felipe. Here they learned that Houston would not make a stand but was bent on a continuation of his retreat. Realizing this, the trouble grew in intensity. Some wanted to go down the river, others demanded to be lead up the stream. This contention assumed a serious phase, but the Commander prevailed, and the army marched up the river to Groce's; and here they remained until April the 13th—Just one month from the time they had set forth in retreat from Gonzales. By this time the fighting force of the army had dwindled to about 500 men; but with the addition of two four-pound cannons,[23] known as the 'twin sisters'—gifts from patriotic citizens of Cincinnati—which had reached the army on a small steamer plying the Brazos.

"The situation grew tense. No one except the Commander and probably a few of his most trusted officers knew the next objective point of the army. That a crisis was approaching, every soldier had reason to believe, from the fact that hourly they were urged to increase their speed. What the army scouts had reported to the commander was kept a profound secret. But the forced march was increased —some said it was a flight from the Mexicans; others said, 'Old Sam' had scented something in the wind and was hastening forward to cut off Santa Anna who was reported to have crossed the San Bernard. However, many of the boys believed that Houston would never halt as long as the road was open to the Sabine. Lack of confidence was manifest, not only in the army, but among the people. In proof of this I cite one instance out of many that occurred during the retreat:

"One night before reaching Harrisburg, the army went into camp near a small farm owned by a man who was then in Captain Mosley Baker's company on detached service. His family remained at home, the brave wife and mother refusing to join in the great exodus known as the 'Runaway Scrape.' The men began tearing down the fences and using the

[23] Parker's, The Texian Revolution, p. 375.

rails for fuel. The woman vainly protested and finally appealed in no mild terms to Houston. 'My good woman,' said the General, 'you see our situation; the men having marched all day through mud and rain, are tired and hungry, and besides your fence rails there is no other wood to be had with which to make fires to cook their rations.' 'Then you'll pay me for my rails,' screamed the exasperated woman. 'Sorry to admit good lady,' said Houston, 'that we haven't a cent, otherwise I would readily pay you for all damages; but I'll tell you what I'll do. When I whip old Santa Anna, I'll be back this way, and I'll have my men make rails and rebuild your damaged fences.' With a look of withering scorn, and shaking her finger defiantly at the General, that brave Texas mother exclaimed, 'You big, cowardly, nasty, old rascal! You'll never come back this way, and you know it; you are running now, like a cur dog, from a gang of thieving Mexicans, and you'll not stop running until you get out of Texas. When you whip Santa Anna! Huh!' For once the General felt defeated and rode away crestfallen. And it is said that when he became President of Texas, he saw that the brave woman was paid well for her rails, and besides sent her a fine clock as a gift.

"The bee-line march from Groce's to Harrisburg was perhaps the most difficult of the entire retreat. Constant rains had made the prairies veritable quagmires, and swollen streams further retarded their progress. An incident is told by an eyewitness, which gives some idea of the difficulties under which the retreat was made, and it illustrates the manner in which the commander handled and controlled his men:

"The road being in bad condition, the wagons frequently bogged; and the infantry marching in the rear of them were not permitted to pass them. At one time the hindmost wagon was completely bogged, and the infantry coming up, sat down besides the road—dozens of them near the wagon. The General, as usual, dismounted to instruct the teamsters.[24] Seeing that the right hand hind wheel had sunk to the hub, he called the seated men to come and raise it, but not one of them moved. Then stuffing his pants into his boots, he said to the teamsters, 'Come, boys, let us see what a few men in extremity can do.' And he and the two teamsters waded in the mud to the mired wheel and took hold of the spokes, telling the driver to pop his whip. 'Look at the General! Look at the General! Look at the General!' shouted the men; and at once more men had crowded around the wagon than could reach it. They lifted the wheel out of the mud and the wagon was soon on firm ground.[25]

And now, while the *relator*, Creed Taylor, is absent from the scene of military activity—but riding hard to join his comrades in arms—is the time to briefly review the movements and situation of the two belligerent armies. The story of the Texas Revolution in its final swing, seems like the closing act of a great drama played on a moving stage.

When Santa Anna invaded Texas in February, 1836, he brought with him his ablest generals and choicest veterans; and in their victorious march the invaders left a trail of blood to mark their route. After the bloody episodes at Bexar and at Goliad, with the incidental destruction of scattered fragments of the Matamoros expedition beyond the Nueces, the

---

(24) I have always understood that Houston served for a time as Wagon Master back in his early years when he was experiencing his first services as a soldier under General Jackson in the United States Army.

(25) This incident was furnished and vouched for by veteran, W. P. Zuber, in his "Recollections of Sam Houston," written expressly for the editor.

dictator was intoxicated with success and prepared to march to the Gulf and the Louisiana border with the same relentless cruelty that had characterized his course all along; and he had every reason to believe that he could achieve an easy conquest with his great army approximating ten thousand soldiers, under trained and brutal commanders, while the Texan force at no time far exceeded one thousand men, poorly equipped and more or less disorderly. But there was a vast difference in the spirit and the motives of the Mexican and the Texan armies.

Santa Anna boastingly called himself the "Napoleon of the West," and he was not without considerable genius as a military man. The disposition of his forces displayed a fairly accurate knowledge of the country and an admirable plan of campaign. In its general features it resembled General Grant's final campaign to subdue the Southern Confederacy. He divided his great army into three columns: the first, under General Gaona, he sent to Nacogdoches by the old Comanche Trail at the upper crossing of the Trinity; the second, under Sesma, was to advance to Bastrop on the Colorado, and thence to San Felipe; Urrea was to command the third column and to scour completely the region between Gonzales and Galveston, while he himself, with Filisola, took two battalions and five pieces of artillery and proceeded directly from Bexar towards the north, intending to join Sesma on the Colorado, it being his purpose to have all troops converge at Galveston at the mouth of the Brazos, whence he would sail for Vera Cruz, after the conquest of Texas, to pose as the victorious President of all Mexico from the Yucatan to Louisana—indeed as the "Napoleon of the West." This superb conception was a masterful and comprehensive plan, but it miscarried and brought disaster upon the invaders—mainly by Santa Anna's own over-confidence and Houston's strategic movements and avoidance of a conflict until the psychological moment.

To meet and defeat the plans of the arrogant dictator, Houston had pursued a Fabian policy, ever retreating, dodging, avoiding an engagement with the enemy's superior force, delaying his own movements in the hope of just such a fortuitous contingency as actually happened and decided the issue. The great Napoleon had a maxim, that success in war depended upon never doing what your adversary expects you to do, and the Texan commander refused to give battle to the Mexicans until the latter concluded that Houston was too weak or too cowardly to risk a combat, and then they rushed onward into the fatal *cul de sac,* where they were forced to fight under very disadvantageous circumstances, although still outnumberng the Texan army at least two to one.

The movements of the two great army chiefs was indeed interesting, and at times exciting, as they marched and maneuvered—matching wits for favorable time and place to battle for the mastery of a fair domain. Two of the most unique chieftains in the military annals of the new world. One carried the simple title of General Sam Houston, commander of the Texan Volunteer Army, the other, with much ego, "General Antonio Lopez de Santa Anna, President of Mexico and Commander of all her Armies." One led a little force of less than a thousand rifle-armed, buckskin clad pioneers struggling for their homes and liberty. The other commanded a well equipped army of eight or ten thousand trained troops, representing a nation of eight or ten million people. The two forces were gradually converging and the crisis was approaching.

The Mexican commander had decided to make the decisive engagement on the Brazos, and was concentrating his forces for that purpose. But when he reached San Felipe (April 7th) and found that Houston had gone up stream, he naturally concluded that the Texans had decided to abandon further resistance to his invasion, and he hastened to end the campaign—countermanding his orders for concentration on the Brazos, and leaving his generals to follow his previously arranged program, while he himself took about one thousand men, with one or two pieces of artillery, and hurried down the river to Harrisburg, which village he burned to the ground. It had been occupied by the government "ad interim," and the officers of the administration barely escaped capture, fleeing to New Washington, on Galveston bay, whither Santa Anna's cavalry pursued them, but they got away in a boat just in time to avoid being made prisoners.

Houston left Donahoe's on the Brazos, April 14th, to follow Santa Anna down the river. Mosley Baker, brave and loyal as he was, though impetuous and unreasonable, had rejoined the army, but Captain Martin had been sent to the east to guard the families of the settlers. The army reached Buffalo Bayou on the 18th, where Deaf Smith, the famous scout, brought in a Mexican courier he had captured, and it was learned for a certainty that Santa Anna was in front of them below Harrisburg. Houston now made a speech to his soldiers, firing them to the greatest enthusiasm and he told them that in the coming battle their war-cry should be, "Remember the Alamo! Remember Goliad!"

On the 19th the force was crossed over the bayou in rickety boats, two miles below Harrisburg, marched all night halting at sunrise on the 20th on the borders of the historic field of San Jacinto. Houston's retreat was at an end.

At this juncture a small party of Rangers, scouting under Captain Robert M. Coleman, had the good fortune to capture a large flat-boat at Lynch's Ferry, loaded with provisions, furnished by Texas Tories for the Mexican army. The boat was quickly towed up the San Jacinto and Buffalo Bayou to the Texan camp. The prize was indeed a valuable and timely one for the poorly provisioned army.

Meanwhile the Mexican general found himself trapped—pocketed in the narrow peninsula below Harrisburg, between the San Jacinto River and Buffalo Bayou, with the Gulf of Mexico at its eastern extremity, and his army of a thousand men isolated entirely from his other troops in the interior. Through his faithful scouts and spies the Texan commander was advised of the enemy's movements and position. It was a perilous position for a commander who had to deal with men like Houston and his soldiers, animated by a passionate desire for revenge. As Houston said, "The enemy is now treading dangerous ground—the soil on which they are to be conquered."

Santa Anna's only route of escape from his perilous situation was by way of Lynch's Ferry, which would compel him to pass almost directly in front of the Texan camp. Now was the time and the situation that Houston had waited for. It is, of course, not to be said that he had expected just such a combination of favorable circumstances to put his wily antagonist at his mercy, but he was quick to see and to take advantage of the opportunity, as its chances of a decisive movement were disclosed to him by his scouts.

As Santa Anna marched up the river he encountered a part of the Texan army, on the 20th, and a sharp skirmish occurred, after which the enemy withdrew towards the San Jacinto and struck camp not far away, on the opposite side of the peninsula from the Texan camp. That afternoon a smart cavalry fight between Lamar's Troopers and the Mexican horse occurred, in which Lamar so distinguished himself for gallantry that he was put in chief command of the Texan cavalry next day. During the night the Mexican extended their lines and threw up temporary breastworks of packs, baggage, brush, and dirt, leaving an opening in the center of their position, for their artillery. The stage was now set for the final act in the drama.

The situation thus chosen for the approaching conflict was admirable. In the rear of the Texan position lay the deep, sluggish waters of Buffalo Bayou; in front for two miles was the rolling surface of the prairie, covered with waving grass and interspersed with clumps of trees, while beyond it stretched the gulf marshes of San Jacinto Bay, miry and treacherous and covered with swamp timber and rank verdure. The Texan camp was chosen just below a rise in the ground that led up to the level of the prairie in front, while immediately in front of the encampment were two small groves of live oaks, with a skirt of timber reaching from the bayou to the top of the rise where the prairie began. It was a sheltered spot, furnishing full advantage for a formation and advance of the little army close upon the enemy.

And just here, on the very eve of the most trying episode in his life, it will be proper to say that General Sam Houston was no coward or weakling. It is related that on the night of the 20th, a council of war was held, at which it was proposed to tear down some vacant houses on the de Zavala ranch and use the timbers of them to make a floating bridge over which the Texan army, in case of defeat in the coming battle, might escape. The General vetoed the suggestion with indignation. "No," he thundered, "we don't want any bridges to escape over; for when we go into battle we are going to fight fast and hard; and, by the eternal God, we are going to win—or die!"

But we anticipate. Let us revert to other gripping and fast occurring events of bloody strife—the most dramatic, the most tragic and the most pathetic scenes in all Texas history, the massacre of the Alamo men, and the slaughter of Fannin's forces.

CHAPTER XIII

Bowie, Crockett, Travis, Bonham Pass in Review

Side lights of history, especially in the form of personal narratives, are always instructive and illuminating. They carry that personal touch and human feeling that stilted history does not possess. From such sources come the most trustworthy accounts of events, the most faithful history of a country. From such sources must come the only reliable story of the Alamo fight. One such narrative has been left to us, told by a reliable eyewitness and participant—the late Dr. John Sutherland, of Sutherland Springs, Texas. It was my good fortune to know Dr. Sutherland, and I have often talked with him and listened to his story of the matchless fight and heroic defense of the Alamo by that devoted little band of immortal heroes. The Doctor was one of the outstanding men of early Texas, and anyone who ever knew that noble patriot and Christian gentleman will vouch for the truth of what he relates.

Dr. Sutherland was a Virginian, born on the River Dan, May 11, 1792, but was reared principally in Tennessee, near the historic Sutherland Ferry over Clinch River. He came of historic and heroic ancestors. In 1835 he was a practicing physician in Tuscumbia, Alabama; but like many other young and patriotic fellows, of the southern states especially, the Texan struggle for liberty kindled his fighting spirit and drew him to the scene of conflict.

Dr. Sutherland was one of the Alamo men who actually (through an accident) escaped to tell something of that heroic episode. His graphic narrative has never before been given the world and will be read with swelling interest. His part in the stirring drama follows:

TALL MEN WITH LONG RIFLES

"Late in 1835, I came to Texas to make it my home and to help in her unequal struggle with the tyrannical powers of Mexico, which terminated in securing for her the liberties we now enjoy.

"Arriving at San Felipe in December and taking the oath of allegiance to the Provisional Government of Texas, I proceeded on in company with Captain William Patten and ten other volunteers, to San Antonio. En route we met General Houston, then in command of the Texas forces, who advised against going on to Bexar, saying that he had ordered all forces to fall back east of the Guadalupe River. We decided however, to go ahead, and arived at San Antonio on the 18th of January, 1836.

"On reaching the old Mexican town, I sought private quarters and was fortunate in securing lodging with Lieutenant Almeron Dickenson and wife who were keeping house there. Here I became acquainted with all the Texans of the place, of whom there were some one hundred and fifty, these being a part of the force that had captured the place from General Cos the month previous. Of that original force, some had returned home to their families, while a large part had gone with Frank Johnson and Dr. Grant on a rampage westward toward the Rio Grande. Their fate is recorded in history.

"The situation I found at Bexar was not very favorable. The forces which had left on the wild goose chase had taken with them almost everything in the way of supplies, and more than their share of the scant supply of clothing, blankets, and medicines. The improvised Texas government was of course unable to furnish further supplies.

"The remaining force lived on cornbread and beef, the latter from a diminishing stock of cattle in the country, and the corn from the very few farmers who irrigated in the vicinity of town. But the consumption of these commodities at Bexar had been so rapid for some months past that both were becoming scarce. The men, mostly volunteers were out of money, and there was no government treasury; they of course had received nothing in the way of pay. Small amounts were obtained from a few patriotic individuals, from time to time, and distributed among those in greatest need.

"This state of affairs, with no prospect of immediate relief, was fast bringing about dissatisfaction among the men. Colonel James C. Niell, in nominal command, readily foresaw that something must be done and that, too, without delay, or his position would be abandoned and subject to be retaken by the enemy, should they return. He therefore determined to procure if possible, a portion of a $5,000.00 donation which had been made to the cause of Texas by Harry Hill, of Nashville, and accordingly left Bexar on the 12th or 13th of February for that purpose.

"Meantime Travis had been commissioned a Lieutenant-Colonel and ordered to raise a regiment of men for the regular service; but rumors coming that the country would soon be invaded, and regarding the maintenance of the force at Bexar as of vital importance, he hastily set forth with about twenty men to join the depleted force at that place. When Neill left Bexar, Jim Bowie assumed nominal command, but he was really a sick man, unable to perform his duties properly, so when his friend Travis arrived he requested him to take command.

"Many errors and unwarranted statements find their way into history through careless chroniclers. Some writers are wont to make it appear that bad feelings and rivalry existed between Travis and Bowie—both red-headed and high strung. When Travis reached Bexar, Bowie gladly conceded to him the supreme command of that post; assuming the position of second in command. Unfortunately, at the beginning of the hasty preparations for defense, Bowie was injured while assisting in the mounting of the artillery. In passing under one of the guns some one let a shot fall, which struck him with such force as to cause him to fall to the ground, striking some object which dislocated his hip and otherwise severely injured him. He continued to hobble around however, and directed preparation, until a piercing norther produced a cold which speedily developed into pneumonia.

"Of the early life of Travis not much is known, and his heroic career in Texas has given careless chroniclers opportunity to write fancy sketches of this immortal hero. One writer says Travis was a foundling; that his middle name was *Bar* instead of *Barrett*, Bar being given him, it is alleged from the fact that he was found tied to the bars of a gate on the farm of a man named Travis, who cared for, adopted, and named him accordingly; all of which is a malicious falsehood, the slanderous story having been invented and circulated by an enemy neighbor of the Travis family through revenge for a fancied wrong.

"Already suffering from tuberculosis, the hero of many desperate combats was forced to take his cot; but throughout the struggle in his half delirious moments he cheered and encouraged his comrades on to the last breath. With supreme effort he arose from his death-couch, pistol in hand, for the final end, and thus sold his life gloriously.

"The combined forces at Bexar now numbered 172, but of these some twenty-five or thirty were on the sick list, and suffering through want of medical aid. The surgeon of the command, Dr. Pollard, had consumed his scant stock of medicine, and no further supply was to be obtained in the country. In this emergency I was requested to take charge of the sick and to appropriate a small quantity of medicines I had brought with me. I did so, and finally succeeded in relieving most of them. A few, however did not recover entirely, one of whom was Colonel Bowie, whose disease being of a peculiar nature, was not to be cured by an ordinary treatment.

"Having taken this hasty view of the situation at Bexar up to the time Travis arrived and assumed command of the post, I will now tell some of the startling incidents that followed in rapid succession. From the time of my arrival at San Antonio until the 23rd of February, I was cognizant of all that occurred of importance in and about the garrison of the Alamo, and remember well the hopes, fears, and anxieties of Travis and his men for the safety of the country. Everyone showed himself a true patriot and in the end proved himself a real hero.

"I propose to state such facts as came within my own personal knowledge up to the time of my departure from Bexar, and such information as I derived from the statements of others who were witnesses to the siege and fall of the fortress. I have frequently conversed with one who was in the Alamo for some days whilst the siege was going on, and with others who were there and witnessed the progress of the struggle from its beginning to its unfortunate termination. The first alluded to was John W. Smith, a noble gentleman whose name deserves a conspicuous place in Texas history. The latter were those who were spared from the massacre—Mrs. Dickenson and Colonel Travis' servant. I had also an interview with Colonel Almonte, General Santa Anna, and his private secretary Ramon M. Caro, all of whose accounts agree in the main with each other. These statements, both Mexican and American, being made separately and at different times, and corroborating each other as they do, build a weight of evidence which is not to be obtained from any other source, and which seems substantial and conclusive. How I escaped the fate of my comrades in the Alamo, through an accidental injury and being sent out by Travis to enlist volunteers, will appear in its proper connection with other incidents I shall relate.

"Previous to the actual arrival of the Mexican army and the beginning of the siege, a very loose military rule existed, Travis exercising very little discipline over his men who loitered about town, passing the time at cock fighting, card playing, and attending fandangos by day and by night. It is proper here to note that while professing friendship to the American troops, very few Mexican citizens of the country were sympathetic to the cause of Texas—a majority occupying a kind of half-way ground, ready to follow the dominant party. It is said that between twelve and fifteen hundred of them joined Santa Anna during his stay in San Antonio, and while on the march from that place to the Colorado.

"From time to time there were rumors of an invasion of the country, but being of an unauthorized character, from Mexican sources, but little attention was paid to them. It was generally believed that Cos' recent signal defeat would serve as a warning to the war lords of Mexico. Although these frequent rumors of a large Mexican army coming soon to conquer the rebellious province, but few felt any alarm. A few did give credence to these reports and realized the possibility and danger of a surprise. One of those was the patriotic Captain Juan N. Seguin, who though he has been charged with traitorous hostility toward the Texans, certainly did not manifest it at the time of which I am speaking. Whatever his attitude and his excuse for his conduct toward Texas at a later period, Seguin certainly proved himself a true friend to Texas at that critical time.

"So strong was Seguin's belief of an early invasion, and as a precaution against surprise, he himself stationed a spy on the Rio Grande, with orders to report immediately any movements which indicated an advance. This spy was a young man named Blaz Herrera, a cousin of Seguin. He remained at his post for some time before any signs of a suspicious nature were discovered. About the 18th of February, however, Santa Anna crossed the Rio Grande into Texas with an army of five or six thousand men. Herrera made inquiry as to their numbers, plans, etc., without being suspected of his motives.

"According to instructions Herrera set out post haste for Bexar, where he arrived about dark Saturday evening, the 20th, and reported his discoveries to Seguin, who immediately informed Colonel Travis of the situation and assured him of his implicit confidence in Herrera. About nine o'clock that night a council of war was held in Colonel Travis' room. Spy Herrera was brought in and reported all he had recently seen and learned; that he had seen the Mexican army cross the river; that the main body of the infantry and the artillery, numbering thirty-five hundred to four thousand, would travel slowly, but that the cavalry, fifteen to twenty hundred strong, would push forward for the purpose of taking the Texans by surprise. This startling news created considerable discussion, some holding that it was the most authentic information that had yet reached them, while others, the majority, declared that it was only the report of a Mexican, and entitled to no more consideration than others of like character that had been frequently circulated through the country. Thus this warning was unheeded and the council adjourned.

"In justice to the incredulous disposition of Travis and his men, it may be stated that such was the universal distrust of Mexicans that no report coming from them received due consideration. So many false alarms had been given by a degraded class of 'greasers' continually passing to and fro, through the country, that no credence was given to any rumor, however plausible, and no immediate danger suspected. Many persuaded themselves that he was afraid to meet American riflemen in mortal combat. 'He knew better.' A majority believed Santa Anna would never attempt to conquer Texas; that Cos' defeat would have the effect to intimidate him from ever attempting again to subdue the country. This will relieve Travis of the charge that he manifested a lack of precaution in neglecting scouting service. Travis had been in the place only a short time, and the men who had been there months showing such indifference to all Mexican reports of invasion, it was natural that he should fall into the same error. Until Colonel Niell's departure, Deaf Smith had been a regular scout, but he had observed nothing of an alarming nature—'All was quiet along the Rio Grande.'

"The first and second days following Herrera's report passed as usual, without the occurence of anything worthy of notice. The little excitement which his report created passed into deeper discredit and the usual air of careless indifference continued.

"On the morning of the 23rd, however, the inhabitants of the place were observed to be in quite an unusual stir. They were hurrying to and fro through the streets, with obvious signs of excitement. Houses were being emptied, and their contents put into carts, and hauled off. Such of the poorer class who had no better mode of conveyance, were shouldering their effects, and leaving on foot. Such peculiar movements elicited investigation. Orders were issued that no others were to be allowed to leave town, which had the effect of increasing the commotion. Several were arrested and questioned as to the cause of the movement, but no satisfactory answer could be obtained—they were 'going into the country to prepare for the coming crop.' Such an excuse was too flimsy to believe. Travis continued to investigate and to take some measures of precaution, lest the enemy actually be approaching.

"Finally Travis was informed, secretly, by a friendly Mexican, that the enemy's cavalry had reached the Leon, eight miles out, on the previous night and had sent messengers to inform the inhabitants to vacate the town at early dawn, as it would be attacked next day. He stated further a messenger had arrived a day or two before, and that it had been the purpose of the enemy to take the Texans by surprise, but in consequence of a heavy rain and muddy roads, their march was impeded, and they were unable to reach the place in time. Yet, in the face of all this, as well as Herrera's corroborated story, the whole thing was countenanced as among the many false rumors. But Travis was ill at ease and exhibited considerable concern. He came to me forthwith, informed me what he had seen and learned, and wished to borrow my horse to send out a party for his caballada pastured, on the Salado, that he might mount and start a scout through the country.

"In company with Colonel Travis, and at his request, I proceeded to post a reliable man on the roof of the old church, as a sentinel, to remain at his post, and to ring the bell, if he should discover any signs which he might deem ominous. Ere long the sentinel rang the bell vigorously, and cried out, 'The enemy is in view.' I immediately ran across the plaza from Nat Lewis' Store, to the church, where a considerable crowd soon gathered around Travis—the Colonel was not excited but he exhibited much concern. Several persons ran up to the sentinel's post, but seeing nothing of the enemy, yelled that it was 'a fake alarm,' and that they believed the whole tale was 'a big lie.' The sentinel exclaimed with an oath that he had seen them, that they had hid behind a brush wood. The crowd disbanded, the greater part discrediting the report altogether.

"At this juncture I proposed to Colonel Travis that if anyone who knew the country, would accompany me, I would go out and ascertain the truth or falsity of the whole matter. John W. Smith was ready to go with me. As I mounted my horse I remarked to Travis, that if he saw us returning in a run, he might be sure we had seen the enemy. This arrangement proved of some benefit. Taking the Laredo road at a moderate gait soon brought us to the top of the slope, about a mile and a half west of town. Here a startling sight met our gaze. We found ourselves within 150 yards of 1500 well-mounted and well-armed Mexican cavalry, their polished armor glistening in the rays of the sun, as they formed in line, behind the chaparral and mesquite bushes, mentioned by the sentinel, the commander riding along the line, waving his sword as though giving orders.

"The sight was really a thrilling one, but of course we did not remain long to view it, but quickly wheeled around and started full speed back to town.

"In consequence of the heavy rain of the preceding night, the road was quite muddy, and my horse being smoothly shod, he began to slip and scramble, and I somersaulted, my gun flying from my hand, and the animal itself falling and rolling directly across my knees. Smith dismounted and succeeded in pulling the horse off me. With Smith's assistance the stunned animal finally managed to regain its feet. Picking up the pieces of my broken gun, and with assistance, I again mounted, and we were not long in reaching town.

"On the civil plaza we met Colonel Crockett and his little party of twelve Tennesseans, who informed us that Colonel Travis had moved his headquarters, together with the entire force from town into the Alamo, and that they were on their way to join him. After crossing the river we met Captain Dimmitt and Lieutenant Nobles. The former inquired where we were going and what we had seen, when he remarked that 'there were not enough men at Bexar to defend the place, that it was bound to fall;' and insisted that I should go with him, saying he 'would see me safely out;' that he would go and bring reinforcements to the garrison.' I replied that I should report to Colonel Travis, and could not say that I could accompany him even then. As we rode on he remarked that he would wait for me down the street at his house.

"It was not until attempting to dismount at headquarters, that I was sensible of the extent of the injury caused by the fall of my horse. On alighting from my saddle my knee gave way, and I fell to the ground. With the assistance of Colonel Crockett I got up and limped to Colonel Travis' room, where we found him writing a dispatch. He had watched our movements, and by this time no longer doubted that the enemy was upon him. I informed him of our discoveries, and of the accident which happened to me, and added that if I could be of any benefit to him I was at his service. He replied that he wished me to go forthwith to Gonzales and rally the settlers, if possible, to his relief. Colonel Crockett, yet standing by, remarked: 'Colonel, here am I, assign me to a position, and I and my dozen Tennessee boys will try to defend it.' Travis replied that he wanted him to defend the picket wall extending from the end of the barracks, on the south side, to the cover of the church.

"At this time the Texans had well nigh consumed everything they had on hand. Grant and Johnson had left them but a small supply of coffee, sugar, and salt, which had long since disappeared, and none of these necessaries were to be found, though they might have had plenty of money with which to buy them. Their meats they obtained by driving beeves from the prairie, just as they needed them, never more than twenty-four hours supply on hand at one time, and at this juncture almost entirely out.

"They were also out of corn with which to make their bread, and had no money to purchase more. But fortune favored. While they were retiring from town to the Alamo, they met 20 or 30 beeves coming down the Alamo street, now Commerce, to the river. All hands gathered around and drove the cattle into the Alamo. A supply of bread also came by chance. During the hurry and excitement of the day, a number of Mexican jacales near the Alamo had been vacated, and in them we found 80 or 90 bushels of corn. These were their supplies during the siege.

"As soon as the Texans entered the Alamo they set about preparing for its defense. The beeves were secured in a pen on the northeast side of the fortress. The corn was stored away in some of the smaller rooms of the barracks. They did not obtain water from the small canal which ran nearby, but dug a well within the walls; it was necessary to arrange to shoot over it. This was done by throwing up an embankment against the walls inside. The guns, of which they had some 30 or 40 pieces of various calibers, among them an eighteen pounder—most of them captured from Cos the previous December—were mounted at the most strategic points, though I do not think that more than twenty pieces were put to use during the siege. From the same source they had obtained a considerable supply of muskets, swords, bayonets, together with any amount of ammunition, which came in good play. All were armed with good rifles, single-barreled pistols, and heavy knives. Their powder was secured in a small room in the southwest corner of the church, which was covered with an arched roof of stone and plastered over perfectly tight, so as to make it proof against sparks of fire from the enemy's shells.

"As soon as Travis ascertained that the enemy was upon him in large force he sent a dispatch to Colonel Fannin, at Goliad, informing him of the condition and requesting assistance, as speedily as it could be sent. This dispatch was borne by a young man by the name of Johnson, and not by J. B. Bonham, as stated in some accounts. On the 23rd, when Almonte arrived at Bexar, Bonham was absent from town. He had visited Texas with a view of purchasing land, and had not attached himself to the army, though he held himself in readiness to serve the country whenever an emergency occurred. At the time the cavalry arrived he was prospecting the country in the vicinity of San Antonio, and on hearing the report of the cannon in town, started on the return. Near the Salado he met Johnson with the dispatch to Fannin and learning the cause of the cannon fire, he put spurs to his horse and made his way into the Alamo.

"Between three and four o'clock, p. m., I set out, as requested by Colonel Travis, for Gonzales. I first rode down the river a short distance, thinking to

TRAVIS DRAWS THE LINE IN THE ALAMO

meet Dimmitt, but he had gone, taking the road to Goliad. Near the ford I fell in with friend J. W. Smith, also on his way to Gonzales. Just then we were paralyzed for a moment when we saw the enemy march into the military plaza in grand order. While we sat on our horses for a moment, watching the movements and maneuvers, Captain Nat Lewis came up on foot. He was also bound for Gonzales with as much of his valuables as he could carry in his saddlebags thrown across his shoulder—leaving his store, a very large stock of goods, a contribution to the enemy.

"We soon parted, Captain Lewis taking one direction, Smith and I another—the old Goliad road running south. But after going about half a mile, to divert the Mexicans who might have seen us, we turned due west into the mesquite and chaparral brush. As we crossed the Gonzales road between town and Powderhouse Hill, we saw three men riding in the distance across the Salado, about a mile and a half from us. They were no doubt a scouting party of the enemy, out for the purpose of cutting off anyone attempting to leave town.

"On reaching the Salado, my injured leg began to stiffen and give such pain that I thought of turning back, and should have done so if Smith had not urged me on, believing that the enemy had already surrounded the fort, for already cannon shots were heard in that direction. Resting a moment, and filling our gourds, which we had just bought of an old Mexican whom we met, we continued on paralleling the road and about a mile from it. Out about sixteen miles, and night coming upon us, we stopped, spread our blankets, and despite my intense pain I was soon fast asleep. That was perhaps the most strenuous and eventful day of my life.

"By daylight on the morrow we were again in

the saddle, and after a hard days ride, and anything else than an agreeable one to myself, we arrived at Gonzales about four o'clock, p. m. As we entered the town we made known our mission, and sent notice to all the neighboring settlements with news of the enemy's arrival, and urging every citizen to hasten to the relief of the besieged. This was on Wednesday, the 24th. By Saturday we succeeded in getting 25 men who were placed under the command of Ensign Kimble. These were principally from Gonzales, men of families and her best citizens. They marched away for San Antonio on Saturday about two o'clock, p. m., with John W. Smith acting as guide. On the Cibolo they increased their force to 32, which number reached Bexar about one o'clock, a. m., Tuesday, the 29th.

"On reaching the suburbs of the town they were approached by a man on horseback, who asked in English, 'Do you wish to go to the fort, gentlemen?' 'Yes,' was the reply. 'Then follow me,' he said, at the same time turning his horse into the lead of the company. At that instant Smith remarked: 'Boys, it's time to be after shooting that fellow,' whereupon the obliging stranger put spurs to his horse, sprang into the thicket, and was out of sight in a moment, before a gun could be got to bear upon him. Some suppose that from his fluency in the English language, that it was no less a personage than General Adrian Woll, who was an Englishman in the Mexican service.

"The little band proceeded silently, in single file, toward the fort, but were soon to be saluted again, though not in so friendly a manner. Notwithstanding that Smith had taken the precaution of sending a messenger ahead, there seemed to have been some misunderstanding as to the direction from which they should approach the walls, for the sentinel not being aware of their presence, fired upon them without hailing. The ball took effect in the foot of one of the men. The mistake was soon discovered, when all went in without further mishap.

"It should be stated that when comrade Smith left to conduct the little band of volunteers into the Alamo, I remained at Gonzales to doctor my injured leg, which was still giving me considerable trouble. Travis had promised that he would fire the big eighteen pounder at sunrise every morning as long as he held out. Messengers rode forth every morning before daylight in the direction of San Antonio, sometimes as far as the Cibolo, to catch the signal. The boom of the big gun rolled across the prairies regularly each day—until the 6th of March, when all was silent. With ears on the ground we listened intently and anxiously, but alas! no signal came, and we feared the worst had come to our countrymen in the Alamo.

"Rumors and reports, mostly through straggling Mexicans, now began to come in that the fortress had finally been taken and its brave defenders put to death. You may imagine the terrible excitement such news created in the little town and settlement. Finally on the evening of the 13th, Mrs. Dickenson with her child and Travis' negro servant, Ben, and Joe, the servant of Almonte, came into the Texan army camp, and confirmed the story of the terrible massacre; also bearing a message from Santa Anna to General Houston, 'that he would be up that way soon to slaughter the whole bunch.' Indescribable grief and wailing now prevailed at Gonzales. So many had lost their loved ones in the Alamo. I am utterly unable to describe the wild and terrible scene, and I hope I may never witness such terrible heart rending scenes again. In this terrible hour General Houston decided to retreat eastward with his little volunteer force, yet scarcely having the semblance of an army.

"As the news of the slaughter of the Alamo men, and the retreat of the Texan army, spread through the western settlements, fear seized the people and soon almost the entire population was in flight eastward—the great 'Runaway Scrape' was on.[26]"

---

[26] Having joined the little Texan army at Gonzales, Dr. Sutherland was sent forward by General Houston, with dispatches for President Burnet. The president appointed him an aide-de-camp and sent him to Groce's Ferry on the Brazos, empowering him to impress all boats passing and to do everything possible to assist the fleeing settlers across the river. The doctor remained in the service of the government until after the battle of San Jacinto. He was long one of the useful and leading citizens of Texas. He died April 11, 1867.

CHAPTER XIV

The Most Heroic Fight In American History

The story of the Alamo fight has been told and retold a thousand times and more, and the names and deeds of these dauntless men who fought to the death will be chronicled in history, sung by poets, and painted by artists to the end of time—a story of heroic bravery and matchless fortitude without a parallel in the world's military annals. Unfortunately there is a dearth of reliable information, the few eye-witnesses—non-combatants—leaving but meager accounts of the terrible combat. Such statements as follow, however imperfect or unsatisfactory, must ever remain as the only source for knowledge of details in the progress of the terrible struggle and the final bloody and tragic ending that can ever be given the world. Before proceeding with such statements as have come down to us we should consider some of the events transpiring and conditions prevailing in and about San Antonio immediately preceding the assault upon the old fortress. In the siege and fall of the Alamo there is glory enough for all the future ages of Texas renown, without the least detraction from the real facts—the truths of history only should be written.

After the surrender of General Cos to the Americans in December, Burleson's men scattered, many, in fact nearly all the Texans, returning to their homes, the leaders hied themselves to the convention at San Felipe and the Volunteers from the states dispersing over the country to occupy various small posts and trading centers. Colonel Wm. B. Travis remained at San Antonio with those under his command who were unable to get away and others who, influenced by a sense of duty, remained under his leadership. Travis opposed Grant's proposed expedition against Matamoros, denounced his usurpation of authority and sent a special courier to Fannin at Goliad urging him to have nothing to do with the expedition and pleading with him to obey Houston and Governor Smith rather than engage in a movement which could result only in defeat and disaster. He commanded, exhorted, expostulated, and threatened those in San Antonio who were led off by Grant's promises but their number was far in excess of those who had remained loyal to his authority, and he found himself without means to enforce his mandates, and he could only stand by and witness the departure of those men who carried away all the best horses and whatever else they could seize, even taking the scanty supply of medicines left by General Cos for the sick and wounded of his army that fell into the hands of the Texans at the surrender of the town.

With those that remained Travis could maintain but a mere semblance of discipline. These men were volunteers from other states, they had been promised a liberal reward for their services and pay-day had never arrived. They were disheartened, discouraged, unable to get away, and consequently abandoned themselves to all excesses of a military post. Gambling, cockfighting, and fandangos were the popular pastimes, and at roll call of the 150 names on the list very often there were not 25 to answer. Travis was helpless but bore with the insubordination of these men, realizing the importance of holding Bexar and hoping that the clash of authority between Governor Smith and the Council would be adjusted and that troops and supplies would reach San Antonio in time to forestall any attempt of the enemy to retake the place.

The arrogance and tyranny of these men under

TALL MEN WITH LONG RIFLES

Travis embittered most of the Mexican population. With most of these men the Mexican was regarded as a common enemy and his property was considered as lawful prey. Grant's followers had despoiled them of all their servicable horses to the extent that when one of Cos' wounded men so far recovered as to be able to undertake the homeward journey, he had to remain, as his friends and sympathizing countrymen in San Antonio could not furnish him a horse to ride out of town. These Mexicans knew of Santa Anna's approach; they knew when his army crossed the Rio Grande; but they kept their own council, trusting to the day when an overwhelming force of their countrymen should drive the obnoxious invaders from their presence. A young Mexican girl who had become the mistress of one of Travis' men told her lover of the approach of the Mexican army but her statement was treated as an idle rumor. Travis had scarcely a sufficient number of horses with which to drive in beef cattle from the range along the San Antonio River and this accounts for the fact that there were no scouts or reconnoitering parties to report the advance of the Mexican army. Early in January Travis had sent a detail as far as 25 miles out in the direction of Laredo with orders to burn all the grass in that part of the country. This order was obeyed and further than that, no precautions were taken against the advance of the invading force.

Witness the consternation of these men when suddenly and without warning they awoke on the morning of February 22nd to behold the Mexican army in battle array at their very doors! The night before, Santa Anna with his army lay in absolute security on the Medina, a few miles from town. His spies entered San Antonio during the night and from their sympathizing countrymen obtained all the information they required. These spies found no picket to challenge their presence and spent most of the night carousing with their newly made friends and on their return were accompanied by several of Cos' convalescent soldiers. When Santa Anna heard their report and finding the way clear he ordered that neither bugle nor drum should sound but that with the utmost silence the army should fall into line and move forward.

Our historians tell us that Santa Anna appeared before the walls of Bexar with an army of 6000 men, the flower of Mexican chivalry, trained officers and seasoned veteran soldiers. Let us examine their statements and, if possible, arrive at just conclusions.

As previously stated, Santa Anna left San Luis Potosi with 6019 men of all arms. His divisions were commanded by the following generals: Mora, Gaona, Tolsa, Andrade, Urrea, besides a number of colonels and captains who held important commands. After leaving San Luis, General Urrea's command was detached and marched to Matamoros, where it crossed the Rio Grande and proceeded to Goliad. Urrea had only 300 in his command when he set out for Matamoros, but before he crossed into Texas his army was strengthened by the addition of other troops and his operations were confined to San Patricio, Refugio and Goliad.

General Gaona's division of 1600 men with two twelve pound cannon and two howitzers, did not reach Bexar until the 8th of March, two days after the fall of the Alamo. General Woll arrived on the 10th and Generals Filisola, Arago, and Andrade, with their respective commands reached San Antonio also on the 10th. Just how many troops composed the command of these generals is not known, but 2000 is a reasonable figure and this being a reasonable low estimate and making all the allowances for deaths from disease and hardships and also for the large number of desertions while en route, Santa Anna could not have had much over 3000 effective troops at the Alamo—about half the number usually credited to him by our historians. In his letter to the Secretary of war, written from San Antonio on February 27th, Santa Anna says he reached that place February 23rd with only the division of General Sesma composed of the battalions of Matamoros, Jiminez, the Dolores Regiment and eight pieces of artillery.

"In telling of the siege and fall of the Alamo," says Taylor, "I shall relate only such facts as were told to me by soldiers who took part in the tragedy and citizens who lived in Bexar and were cognizant of all that transpired during those eventful days. True, these were Mexicans but I accepted no narrative as related without corroborative evidence ,and the facts herein recorded were substantiated by the statements of a numbe rsufficient to guarantee the veracity of these statements.

"The 24th of February was spent in preparation for the siege and in reconnoitering the Alamo and its fortifications. Santa Anna knew that Travis' only hope was to hold the Alamo until reinforcements, which he expected daily, could reach him. The Mexican general knew as well as Travis, perhaps better, that the latter's only means of relief lay with Fannin at Goliad. His spies and swift couriers kept him posted as to Fannin's movements, his attempt to leave Goliad for Bexar, his signal failure, and his return to La Bahia. Santa Anna knew all this and, furthermore, he knew that Urrea, with a large force, was moving upon Goliad and that it was only a question of time as to the destruction of Fannin's army.

Hence, all he had to do was to lay siege to the Alamo and by slow degrees reduce the beleagured men to a state of starvation and non-resistance, after which the taking of the fortress would be an easy task.

"During the night of the 24th, two batteries commanding the Alamo were planted, and at dawn on the morning of the 25th these opened fire on the garrison which in turn responded with vigor. A brisk fire was maintained by both sides during the day until late in the evening firing ceased and a deep silence fell upon the town and fortress. During the night, according to my informant, Juan Ortega, who was a sergeant in the Dolores Regiment, and who died at Brownsville in June, 1862, and his story was corroborated by several others whom I knew personally, two entrenchments were constructed along the alameda of the Alamo and, while details of men were working on these entrenchments, nine men came over from the fortress and asked to be conducted into the presence of Santa Anna. As the General was asleep at that hour and no one cared to disturb his slumbers these men were held under guard until morning. Señor Ortega told me that one of these men spoke Spanish sufficiently fluent to make their wants known, but he did not learn whether they were Texans or volunteers. What they said to Santa Anna, when led into his presence, is not known, but it is well attested that they told him where fifty American rifles had been left in town by Travis' men, besides other belongings, all of which were seized by the Mexicans. What became of these traitors I have never been able to learn. Captain Henry Teal, who was one of the commissioners sent by Houston with a copy of the Santa Anna treaty for Filisola's signature and ratification, overtook the retreating Mexican army west of Goliad. He told me, on his return, that he saw four Americans with

Filisola's men. They were not soldiers nor were they prisoners, and appeared to be either fugitives or camp followers. He tried to learn something of their identity and of their antecedents, but they refused to divulge anything and tried in every way to avoid his presence. Teal had heard of the desertions at the Alamo and he believed that these four men were of the nine traitors.

"Of the 38 captives taken out and shot at Ceralvo in 1846, one of them was evidently an American and John McPeters, of Mustang Gray's company, questioned this man on the way to the place of execution but he denied being other than a 'puro Mexicano.' We were told on the day following that this man was indeed an American, that he was a refugee, and with others had come from San Antonio with the Mexican army when it retreated from Texas, and dared not return to his country.

"The desertion of these nine men at the very beginning of the siege of the Alamo was known to all the Mexicans of San Antonio at the time. Owing to the disrespect touching the rights of property displayed by the Americans after the surrender of Cos and up to the date of Santa Anna's arrival, the Mexican population held the utmost hatred toward them, and when these nine came over to Santa Anna and declared their loyalty and fealty their protestations only served to intensify the contempt of these people. This hatred on the part of the populace was fully displayed when Santa Anna ordered the bodies of the Alamo victims burned, many of those people volunteering to gather wood from a nearby chaparral.

"Another American traitor of whom little is known, was one Davis who belonged to General Sesma's command and was colonel of the Queretaro Battalion and took an active part in the storming of the Alamo. I made diligent inquiry among the Mexicans of my acquaintance but no one could tell me anything other then that Davis was an American and was held in favor by Santa Anna. Juan Seguin held the opinion that he was one of those daring Americans who fought with Peter E. Bean against the Spaniards during the war for Mexican Independence and when that was established he accepted a commission in the army, became a naturalized citizen and remained in the service of his adopted country. Filisola mentions this Colonel Davis but once in his account of the Texas invasion.[27]

" 'Thermopylae had its messenger of defeat, but the Alamo had none.' Of course, I was not in the Alamo during the siege and fall, else I would not be here to tell of my humble part in other affairs; and, strictly speaking, the Alamo, unlike Thermopylae, had no messenger of defeat, for certain it is that not one remaining there until the commencement of the final assault escaped or was spared—not one save the few non-combatants, Mrs. Dickenson and babe, Travis' and Bowie's negro servants, and perhaps one or two other servants, to bear to Houston and his little army the news of the bloody tragedy and threats of a like fate.

"I never saw the man Rose, who, it is said, escaped before the Alamo fell: never heard of him until of late years. Of course it is possible that the story is true, but it is more probable that Rose was an impostor and palmed off his story on the confiding Zubers who gave it publicity.

"Another claimant who has succeeded in imposing upon the credulous public and gaining some notoriety was an old Mexican midwife by the name of Candelaria, whose story has found its way into history. She claimed to have been in the Alamo as the nurse

(27) Filisola, Guerra de Tejas.

of Jim Bowie, when it fell. But, mind you, she did not make this claim till in late years when there were few, if any, of her generation left to refute her pretentions. I knew Madam Candelaria as early as the 50's and, while I knew she had spent her life in San Antonio, I never heard of her being in the Alamo during the fight, until a few years ago. The Madam got to be very old, she needed alms and to that end some enterprising but unscrupulous writer helped to prepare her story. I believe it all a hoax.

"Several aged Mexicans yet survive in San Antonio who claim to have been living there when the siege occurred, among others one Juan Diaz, then a youth, the son of Antonio Diaz, the then trusted custodian of San Fernando Cathedral. Juan Diaz is considered an honorable and reliable Mexican, being a native of San Antonio, a man of some prominence, and he is one of the very few survivors of the Mexican Society. An excellent oil portrait of this venerable Mexican hangs in Benevolence Hall, San Antonio.[28] I give his story in substance as he told it to me, and for what it is worth: 'There was much excitement in town as Santa Anna's great army approached and as a boy I observed what was going on. I witnessed and well remember the wonderful sight as the troops, horse and foot, and artillery, swept into town led by the regimental band playing the liveliest airs, and accompanied by a squad of men bearing the flags and banners of Mexico and an immense image that looked like an alligator's head. The band stopped on Main Plaza and remained there until after the fall of the fort; the artillery was parked where the French building now stands, and the canoneers had a clear sweep to the Alamo, there being no buildings at that time between it and the cathedral. I knew of the progress of the siege from

---

(28) Antonio Diaz died several years ago.

day to day; watched some of the assaults from a safe vantage point, and then witnessed the final scene of the bloody drama—the burning of the dead. I did not go out to where the dead were burned; I had no desire to see the great funeral pyre, but the odor of it permeated every part of the town. It was sickening, and for weeks and months people shunned the place. Some of the men who witnessed the cremation said that the Texan and Mexican slain were piled in a heap and burned together.'

"Non-combatants who were in the fortress and spared have left very little of the details. Mrs. Susan Dickenson, wife of the brave Lieutenant Almaron Dickenson, said that the final struggle lasted more than two hours; that the noise of the battle was terrific as the desperate fight went on from every direction, and that the bloody scene was sickening and heart rending. It must have been enough to dethrone the poor woman's reason at that hour, and crouched with her babe in a secluded angle of the church, she knew but little of what was going on in and around the old fortress.'

"I have talked with a few Mexicans who saw service under Santa Anna and fought at the Alamo. Just before the Civil War a Mexican gentleman was passing through the country going from Matamoros to Austin on some business errand. He was traveling in an ambulance accompanied by three or four companions, and one night he encamped on the San Domingo Creek. Here he was attacked and robbed by outlaws that occasionally infested that section, and during the fight he was shot through the arm below the shoulder. He came next day to my ranch in Wilson county and remained a week, doctoring his wound. He had been a captain in the Mexican army and was at the storming of the Alamo. He related many incidents in connection with the battle,

CROCKETT IS THE LAST SURVIVOR OF THE ALAMO

TALL MEN WITH LONG RIFLES

but most of them have passed out of my memory. I remember his effort to say "Crockett" but he invariably pronounced it 'Kwokety.' He said Crockett was the last man slain and that he fought like an infuriated lion. He stated that his last stand was in a small room and with gun in hand he brained every Mexican that tried to enter the door. He used his gun as a club until a shot from just without the door broke his right arm, and his gun-barrel (the stock had been broken off) fell to the floor. Seeing this the Mexican soldiers made a rush into the room with fixed bayonets, but drawing a large knife with his left hand he rushed upon his assailants and, parrying their thrusts, killed several before he was finally slain. He said he did not hear of a sick man being bayoneted while helpless on his bed (Bowie) but there was a sick man who got out of his bed when the Mexicans entered the fortress and died fighting with the rest. He also stated that Santa Anna could not have done otherwise than to put the defenders of the Alamo to the sword, since they were in open rebellion, held a government fortress, and had refused all overtures looking to a surrender.

"While guarding prisoners at Saltillo shortly after the battle of Buena Vista I talked with two of them who were at the storming of the Alamo, and their version was along the same lines as that given by the wounded captain at my ranch.

"An old Mexican by the name of Rodriguez, who lived in Bexar all his life, told me that during the siege of the Alamo the Mexican women in San Antonio remained indoors, praying, and when the final assault began on Sunday morning, every woman was on her knees pleading for the repose of the fallen, foes as well as friends. He spoke of one young woman who was enamored of one of the garrison and who went into the Alamo when the carnage had ceased, found the object of her affection among the slain, folded his hands across his breast, wiped the grime from his pallid face, placed a small cross on his breast, and when ordered away, she dipped her handkerchief in his blood and carried it away in her bosom.

"I was told by a number of San Antonio Mexicans that many of Santa Anna's men deserted after the fall of the Alamo. They told their friends that if all Texans fought like those who fell in the Alamo, they could never expect to return to their homes and there were not enough men in all Mexico to subdue *estos Tejanos diablos*.

"We will never know, of course, just how many of the enemy fell in the Alamo siege and fight, but taking statements of Mexican participants themselves and all other evidence, a conservative estimate would be about 1600 to 2000, or about one-half of the besieging force. Speaking of the Toluca Battalion Santa Anna says: 'They commenced to scale the walls and suffered severely. Out of 800 men, only 130 were left alive.' Such was the fearful execution by iron-willed and steady nerved riflemen and gunners, who, cool and fearless, met the legions and sold their lives dearly.

"Of incidents in the final struggle and of closing scenes in the Alamo tragedy, we know nothing except the little that has been told to us by Mexican participants and eyewitnesses.

"Señor Don Rafael Soldana was a captain in the Tampico battalion and led his company in the final charge on the Alamo on that memorable Sabbath morning. I became acquainted with Captain Soldana at Corpus Christi shortly after the close of the Mexican War and from him I heard the story of the last charge. 'During the siege,' said he, 'which began on the 23rd of February, every available means was employed to harass and weaken the defenders of the fortress. One of the measures employed was that of constant alarms during the hours of the night. At intervals, when silence reigned over the Alamo and all was still in camp, the artillery would open, a great shout would be raised by the besieging forces and this uproar, supplemented by volleys of musketry, was intended to make the impression that a night assault had been planned, and also to make it appear to the beleaguered that their expected reinforcements, while trying to make their way into the Alamo, had become engaged with the enemy and were being destroyed. These continued—almost hourly—alarms throughout the night were supposed to keep every American in position ready to repel the attack, thus through loss of sleep and increasing anxiety unfitting him for the final struggle.'

" 'These men,' said Captain Soldana, and his story was corroborated by others with whom I talked, 'were defiant to the last. From the windows and parapets of the low buildings, when taunted by the Mexican troops, they shouted back their defiance in the liveliest terms. A tall man, with flowing hair, was seen firing from the same place on the parapet during the entire siege. He wore a buckskin suit and a cap all of a pattern entirely different from those worn by his comrades. This man would kneel or lie down behind the low parapet, rest his long gun and fire, and we all learned to keep at a good distance when he was seen to make ready to shoot. He rarely missed his mark and when he fired he always rose to his feet and calmly reloaded his gun seemingly indifferent to the shots fired at him by our men. He had a strong, resonant voice and often railed at us, but as we did not understand English we could not comprehend the import of his words futher than that they were defiant. This man I later learned was known as "Kwockey" (Crockett).

" 'When the final assault was made upon the walls these men fought like devils,' continued Señor Soldana. When asked if any begged for quarter he replied by saying that he had never heard that any of them offered to surrender or that a single man had begged for his life. "Kwockey" was killed in a room of the mission. He stood on the inside to the left of the door and plunged his long knife into the bosom of every soldier that tried to enter. They were powerless to fire upon him because of the fact that he was backed up against the wall and, the doorway being narrow, they could not bring their guns to bear upon him. And, moreover, the pressure from the rear was so great that many near the doorway were forced into the room only to receive a deadly thrust from that long knife. Finally a well directed shot broke this man's right arm and his hand fell useless at his side. He then seized his long gun with his left hand and leaped toward the center of the room where he could wield the weapon without obstruction, felling every man that came through the doorway. A corporal ordered the passage cleared of those who were being pressed forward, a volley was fired almost point blank and the last defender of the Alamo fell forward-dead.

"Señor Soldana told me there were three or four Mexicans who went down with Travis in the Alamo. He did not know of any Mexican women being in the fortress when it fell. He had heard that nine men deserted Travis before the Alamo was invested but he did not see them and did not know what became of them."

"A glamor of romance and chivalry hangs around the story of the Alamo and its immortal defenders; and its heroic defense and fall are among the imperishable records of human fortitude and valor in all ages and countries. Travis, Bowie, Bonham, and Crockett were the noble figures in that terrible sacrifice, but every one of the devoted little band, privates as well as officers, deserves to be canonized in the calendar of heroism so long as valor and the deeds of war are esteemed the test of a patriotism that renders life for love of country. They died at the dawn of Sunday, March 6, 1836, and it is a grim irony of their lonely isolation in the hour of doom that they fell beneath the flag of Constitutional Mexico while, unknown to them, their countrymen at old Washingon-on-the-Brazos had declared the independence of Texas and raised the banner of the 'Lone Star' just four days before.

"The final assault which began before daylight, ended about sunrise, and then, as some one has so pathetically said, 'A stillness fell upon the scene so profoundly that the drip, drip, drip of heroic blood could be heard.' When all was over Santa Anna strode over the scene and then gave orders for the disposition of the dead. The Mexican officers received burial but most of the Mexican privates were either dumped into the river or burned. The bodies of the Texans were gathered up and carted off a short distance where they were thrown into a heap, alternate layers of wood and bodies being placed together and kindling distributed throughout.

"The pile being completed about five o'clock in the evening, it was lighted. Thus was reared the altar upon which the heroic sons of freedom were consecrated to their country. As the flames crackled and increased, the smoke of the sacrifice ascended on high invoking the wrath of the Almighty upon the oppressors, and while the rising incense floated around the throne of heaven the retributive arm of offended justice was lifting the sword of vengeance which fell so heavily upon them at San Jacinto.

"Thus I have attempted to tell the story of the Alamo, a story that will emblazon the pages of history until the end of time, and the spark of patriotism will always enkindle and thrill at the very mention of that fearful conflict—the warm blood rushing to the heart as one listens to the valorous deeds of those matchless heroes in that unparalleled struggle. Indeed, the story of how Travis and his little band of devoted and defiant comrades offered up their lives, a willing sacrifice and a rich oblation upon the altar of Texan liberty at the Alamo fortress in the historic and blood-stained old town of San Antonio, possesses an interest for the reader over any other chapter in the fiery history of Texas. As boys we all remember the charm that possessed us in reading of the wonderful exploits and chivalric acts of prowess performed by Travis, Bowie, Crockett, Bonham, and others of that dauntless band, especially of Davy Crockett and Jim Bowie whose lifeless and mangled bodies were found with heads of dead Mexicans piled high around and upon them—so the story always went.

"'Thermopylae had its messenger of defeat; the Alamo had none.' An this is true as to actual combatants. But there were a few non-combatants within the walls of the doomed fortress, who witnessed the terrible fight from the first shot to the last sword thrust. These were spared, to carry the news of the tragedy to the world.

"Of all the scenes and incidents connected with the fall of the Alamo, it always seemed to me that the story of Mrs. Dickenson and babe is the most pathetic. True, they were spared from the slaughter, but the horrible scenes of blood and carnage through which that devoted wife and mother passed in the fearful hour must have made an impression that haunted her throughout life and left a sadness that never could be erased from her memory.

"As stated, the only inmates of the doomed fortress spared were a few non-combatants, Mrs. Dickenson and child, Travis' negro Ben, and Bowie's colored servant, and perhaps one or two Mexican women, nurses.

"Mrs. Dickenson, as a young mother, had gone into the Alamo with her husband, Lieutenant Dickenson, and with her baby remained with him to the end. Dickenson was a volunteer from Gonzales, and was one of the dauntless men who stood by Travis, Crockett, Bonham, and the others of that 'devoted little band' and went down with them in the holocaust of carnage, fire and death. In telling of the final terrible scenes of that awful combat she could never recount the story without a shudder and without evincing great emotion. Of the last moments she said: 'Finally my husband rushed into the baptismal room of the church, where I stood holding our baby, and exclaimed: 'Great God, Sue! The Mexicans are inside our walls! All is lost! If they spare you, save my precious child!' Then with a parting kiss, he drew his sword and plunged into the strife that was raging in the different parts of the fortification. At this moment poor Jim Bowie, sick unto death, attempted to rise from his cot and follow, but was restrained by his Mexican nurse. When the Mexicans poured into the room I closed my eyes and knelt in prayer. There was much noise and confusion as the assailants crowded around Bowie and the poor man met his death fighting to the last breath.' Thus this poor bereft woman, praying and clasping her baby close to her breast in that terrible hour of mortal combat, witnessed the furious and bloody struggle.

"Mrs. Dickenson was spared and with her baby

came out of that baptism of flame and smoke, which marked the circular zone of hell, with which the bloodthirsty and self-styled "Napoleon of the West" had encircled the doomed garrison on that chill March night of 1836—to be sent out, after the carnage was over and the smoke of the sacrifice had ascended to heaven, as *a messenger of defeat* to bear the fearful tidings of the tragic episode to General Houston.

"If memory serves me right, I first met that historic child and protege of the 'Texas Republic'—Angelina Dickenson, better known as 'the Babe of the Alamo'—at a 'big-to-do' in celebration of the completion of the Houston and Texas Central Railroad to Cypress, near Navasota, in 1856. The affair had been extensively advertised in the newspapers, which brought throngs of 'fair women and brave men' from almost every part of the State, to be the guests of Paul Bremond, the noted financier and promoter of that pioneer railroad of Texas. A big barbecue and ball was given, and I remember many noted Texans vied with each other in gliding with the 'Babe of the Alamo' through the mazes of the dreamy waltz, or in keeping step and places in the old fashioned square dances. She was then light hearted, rosy cheeked, vivacious and beautiful, and was the recipient of many courtesies and much attention. Only twenty years before, the thrilling tragedy of the Alamo had been enacted, and it was yet fresh in the minds of the people. The names and exploits of its heroic defenders had not been forgotten, and anything connected with or pertaining to those dismal days in which they had struggled, suffered and died, was of interest to the liberty loving inhabitants.

"Some two or three years later I again met the 'Babe of the Alamo.' She did not look so fresh and attractive as when I first met her at the great fete. Her greeting was less cordial, and shadows were lurking on the surface of the broad, smooth, open forehead. An anxious and at times a pained expression would creep over her face, and there was a listlessness and signs of languor perceptible in the dark eyes—the rosy cheeks and lips were faded.

"Through the efforts of the Honorable Guy M. Bryan (nephew of Stephen F. Austin) and one or two other patriotic old Texans, a bill was introduced in the Texas Legislature in behalf of this 'child of the state.' The bill was passed; she was educated at the expense of the state, I believe, but as to her subsequent career, I know nothing save from hearsay. I was told that she fell; became a camp-follower during the Civil War, and found an unknown grave. Because of her being the 'Babe of the Alamo' and a precious heritage of the Texas Revolution, caused the hand of charity to draw the mantle of silence as to her sad fate."

CHAPTER XV

Santa Anna Vows to Exterminate the Texans

The Mexican army of invasion entering Texas in February, 1836, moved in two divisions, Santa Anna, chief in command, marching from Laredo up the Rio Grande, thence northward and directly upon San Antonio—the column of General Urrea traveling from Matamoros in the direction of Goliad, diverging to Refugio. Santa Anna's object was to form a junction with Urrea if necessary, to devastate the country and "to permit no Anglo-Americans to settle in Texas." He had already raised the black flag and vowed his determination to exterminate every armed American found in the province.

After the annihilation of Grant's and Johnson's forces as we have seen—the former while boldly scouring the cacti-prairies bordering the Rio Grande in quest of mustangs for army mounts, and the latter while corralling his caballada at San Patricio—Urrea moved forward to engage Fannin at Goliad, going via Refugio, lest a contingent of the enemy escape his fury at that point. At this juncture colonists in the vicinity and a few refugees from San Patricio had sought safety within the ponderous three-foot stone walled mission church—"Our Lady of Refuge." Among the families thus imperiled was that of Louis Ayer, an early and worthy settler of that vicinity, and then serving as Assistant Quartermaster General under Fannin.

At Ayer's request, Fannin ordered Captain Aaron B. King, with his gallant little company of twenty-eight men, to escort the refugees to Goliad. King reached Refugio on March 12th, entered the church-fort, loopholed the walls, barricaded all doors and windows, and made other hasty preparations for defense. As the advance cavalry of the army arrived, making desultory attacks and hovering around awaiting reinforcements, and deeming the situation alarming, King dispatched a messenger who bravely dashed out under cover of night and rode swiftly to "Fort Defiance," telling of the perilous situation and begging for aid. Fannin could ill afford to spare a man from his little force at this critical time, but the appeal was urgent and by midnight of that same day Major Ward, with 100 men, was en route at double quick time, for Refugio and effected entrance into the besieged church at dawn and a little in advance of the arrival of the enemy in full force.

There has ever been a lamentable want of particulars and details bearing upon the tragedy at Refugio, and the little material the historian has been able to collect is composed of disjointed—and in some instances of minor importance—slightly contradictory statements of the very few who escaped, men whose brawny hands were far more deft with the rifle than with the pen.

In view of this scarcity of well connected accounts of military operations around Refugio I submit that given by Filisola, the Mexican historian of the expedition under General Urrea, bearing upon the Refugio affair, which the intelligent reader will accept with a sense of misgiving in certain particulars, since all the authors of that nationality, as is well known, are not exempt from national pride which leads them to the extreme in exaggeration, and ofttimes painting signal defeat in the gaudy colors of a glorious victory. The Mexican historian says in substance:

"On the 12th of March, General Urrea set forth with his entire command, from San Patricio in the direction of Mission del Refugio, situated between Copano and Goliad, leaving San Patricio in military possession of its native male population who were of Irish birth, and 30 of whom accompanied General Urrea's command. On the eve of the departure General Urrea received a communication from the commander-in-chief (Santa Anna) in reply to the former's report of the capture of Grant and the taking of San Patricio, in which communication Urrea was complimented on behalf of the nation for his splendid achievements. He was also instructed to continue his march and was authorized to provide subsistence for his army by seizing the herds of the colonists and whatsoever supplies they might possess, needful for the maintenance of the troops.

"On the 13th Urrea received notice that a strong detachment of the enemy had advanced to the relief of Copano and would stop at Refugio, whereupon the general decided to attack them. To this end he ordered a company under Captain Pretalia, and 30 volunteers from Goliad under command of Don Guadalupe Santos, to go forward with all dispatch, find the enemy and entertain them until he, Urrea, could bring up his command. After this advance party had set off, the general placed himself at the head of 200 cavalry and 200 infantry, with one cannon, and took up the march, leaving the rest of his command in camp on the Arroyo Aransas. After an all-night march without a moment's halt, he reached Mission Refugio at dawn on the following morning, finding the enemy to the number of 100, fortified in the church. Besides these in the church, about 50 lay in ambush off to the left, distant one fourth of a league. These were immediately cut off by the Guanajuato Cavlry.

"Seeing this movement, the enemy formed in front of the church separating a troop of about

30 for the protection and safe delivery of three barricas (casks) of water, drawn by oxen from the river at a point as yet hidden from our view. This movement brought on the action, the general considering it of unmost importance to deprive the enemy of this supply of water, and to that end he ordered forward three detachments which with great courage rushed upon the enemy, captured the casks of water and drove the filibusters back into the church, which was immediately surrounded. Shut up in this edifice the enemy poured a steady fire upon our troops who did not have the prudence to withdraw until they had advanced to within less than 30 *varas* of the church and had exhausted their ammunition. The action was brief but during this short time we were exposed to the enemy's sharpshooters, suffering considerable damage and without possibly inflicting retribution, since those serving the cannon which had been brought into action and placed so as to play upon the church, had been forced to abandon it. Our troops were forced to fall back and it became evident that a strong reinforcement would be required to retrieve the cannon, which was accomplished with considerable loss.

"Although at the beginning of this action only three parties went to the attack as soon as the enemy was shut up in the church, the reserve of our infantry and a part of the Cuantla cavalry advanced dismounted, (all however, was in vain—de baldo) in their strong position, the enemy impudently laughed at our want of caution and they made us pay dearly for our temerity, our loss being thirteen killed and 43 wounded—among these, four officers—while only one of the filibusters was wounded and none killed.

"Realizing the situation General Urrea sent a

courier to Colonel Francisco Garay to hasten forward with all his available forces, from Arroyo Aransas, leaving at that point everything calculated to embarrass his march. Garay arrived at five o'clock in the evening and with the combined forces Urrea advanced upon the grove of timber in which the fifty filibusters were yet posted. An attack from all sides was promptly made and the enemy dislodged before nightfall, killing five of their number and taking two prisoners; our loss being three killed and ten wounded. After being routed the enemy was pursued by the armed country-men (paisanos) from Goliad, who accompanied us, and on the following morning they captured 36 of them, the latter offering no resistance having exhausted their ammunition the evening before.

"Our infantry camped that night in front of the mission, and in spite of being molested from time to time by the discharge of our cannon, did not return the fire but succeeded in setting fire to certain houses that surrounded the church, and in which our troops had found shelter during the morning's action. General Urrea with all his cavalry took position behind the village and maintained a close watch over the road leading to Goliad, and to intercept any reinforcements that might be sent from any point and also to prevent the escape of any one from Refugio.

"A little past mid-night, a prisoner captured by the advance guard was brought to Colonel Garay who at first drew the conclusion that he was one of those driven from the grove of timber, but he proved to be a courier sent from Goliad by Fannin. On his person was found a note from Fannin to Colonel Ward, directing the latter to evacuate, on the moment, the position he occupied at Refugio, at whatever sacrifice, or whatever obstacles might be in the way and without detention to hasten with his command to Fort Defiance (Goliad) where, without fail, he would expect him the following day.

"Estimating the service it would render Colonel Ward on receiving this note, Colonel Garay, without consulting his commander-in-chief, not knowing where he might be found at that hour, released his prisoner and, feigning utter ignorance of the contents of the note, allowed him to proceed to Colonel Ward.

"Having been informed of the enemy's strength that same night and their scarcity of water and provisions, Urrea drew the inference that they would of necessity, on the next day make a determined rally for the purpose of reuniting with Fannin. To guard against this he placed parties of obstruction at all points where he thought the enemy would attempt to pass in their flight, but through failure in placing someone at a point which experience showed was necessary to cover, or else for want of vigilance on the part of the parties so stationed, the result was that during the night which was very dark, and in which a violent norther accompanied by abundant rain, the enemy set forth without their movement being observed by our troops, the cause of this being the fatigue and weariness to which they had yielded as they had marched all the previous night and day without having taken food or refreshment of any kind.

"The next morning General Urrea drew near the church and finding it abandoned by the enemy, ordered it occupied. In the building were found four families of the colonists, six of their wounded, and some Mexicans who had been forced to join the rebel ranks. Reinforcing the guards on the roads leading to Copano and Goliad, the general ordered the cavalry in immediate pursuit; the enemy was overtaken, 16 were killed and 31 prisoners captured.

"Following the action at Refugio, General Urrea left his wounded and equipage in the custody of Colonel Vara, whom he placed in observation over Copano, with a force sufficient to carry into effect the orders given him by the general. Urrea then set out at the head of 200 men, cavalry and infantry, in the direction of Goliad, having sent forward his scouts in the direction of that village. The parties which had been dispatched to scour the adjacent vicinities brought in 14 prisoners and also intercepted a communication from Colonel Fannin, from which it was learned that it was evident that the chief was arranging to evacuate Goliad and retire with his forces in the direction of Victoria, for the execution of which plan his only hope lay in the recruiting with his command the two hundred men under the command of Colonel Ward, who had already suffered the consequences of the action at Refugio. In virtue of this information, the general ordered Captain Don Jose Irracta, with 60 men, to move forward to a position between Victoria and Goliad in order that he might cut off the retreat of the enemy in that direction.

"The fatigue of the troops incident to the long and continued march, the number of prisoners which had greatly increased and the small means available to hold them in custody and to supply them with food and other necessities and in view of the final orders of the Supreme Government and those of the general-in-chief, (Santa Anna) yielding to all these most difficult circumstances although contrary to his own sentiments and purposes, General Urrea was obliged to order the execution of 30 of these adventurers (aventureros) that had been taken with arms in their hands during the late action, at the same time liberating certain colonists and Mexicans that had been found with them.

"This action (the shooting of these prisoners) as well as others to which we will refer, has been made the grounds of reproach heaped upon General Urrea without regard to a circular from the Supreme Government ordering the summary execution of those infamous vandals who were taken with arms in their hands and were profaning the territory with their presence and shedding Mexican blood. Urrea had no authority to overstep these orders, which under the circumstances necessitated the shooting of certain men who were fighting under no recognized flag, assassinating detached parties of Mexicans, burning houses, appropriating the property of the lawful owners—pacific citizens—and moreover, aiming to rob the nation of a great part of her territory. The war of Texas was exceptional; it was not a civil war, neither was it a war of nation against nation; there the robber fought against the proprietor, the assassin against his benefactor, and nothing more natural than to extirpate these hordes of robbers and assassins. Therefore there was no reason for the attempt to inculpate General Urrea, who acted, not in conformity to his own sentiments of humanity, but under orders of his superiors.[29]"

The movements and fate of Captain King and party may now be briefly noted. On this point some confusion and discrepancy exists among writers. There were but few witnesses spared from whom the facts could be learned. One, Captain Henry Scott, a mere lad, who then and long after, lived at Refugio, witnessed the bloody scenes, and he represents that a controversy arose between Ward and King as to who should command and that bad feel-

[29] References: Relacion de Don Francisco Garay. Memorias para la Guerra de Tejas, Filisola, Vol. 2, pp. 410-419.

ings resulted. And this may account for the separation of the two companies at such a critical time. One of our historians[30] says, "King suicidally refused to serve under Ward, who, having now but 107 men, was soon attacked and forced to retreat into the church-fort, from which he had just released King (King in the meantime having left the place, followed 18 of Ward's men to destroy some ranches, whose owners had shown hostility to the Texan cause).

"Ward fought gallantly till night against Urrea's whole force, killing many Mexican soldiers, and then, his ammunition almost exhausted, eluded the enemy and retreated across the prairie toward Victoria.

"King, wandering around in a confused way, was surrounded the next morning and compelled to surrender with all his men, 46 in number (only two had been killed) and all save two Texans who escaped during the slaughter, were brutally shot to death."

After Ward's retreat King and his company, it seems, reentered the fort. Veteran R. N. Hill, another youthful inmate of the Refugio church and companion and playmate of Henry Scott, thus tells of their fate:

"On the morning after Ward's retreat, Captain King surrendered with his command as prisoners of war. His men filed out and laid down their arms, and the Mexicans entered the church. The first sight that met their eyes was the three wounded men left by Ward. They were mercilessly butchered by the Mexican officers as they lay on their beds unable to rise.

"Captain King and his men (with the exception of one man, spared) were marched out on the road to Bexar, about one mile, where they were halted,

---

(30) John Henry Brown, "History of Texas," Vol. 1, p. 600.

ordered to face about and kneel. They were about to comply, when one of the poor men called out: 'Boys, we are to be murdered; let's face the cowards and die on our feet.' They refused to turn and were shot down as they stood; and to make sure, each one afterwards had a lance run through his body. The writer stood in the window of the church, to see the men start for Bexar, and was a witness to the whole scene at a distance of about a mile. These are my recollections of this massacre.[31]

(31) Veteran R. N. Hill—Letter dated Galveston, May 21, 1859, published in the Texas Almanac for 1859.

CHAPTER XVI

A Famous Hero Comes Upon the Scene

Among the heroes of the Texas Revolution the name of Colonel Fannin will always stand out in emblazoned letters on the pages of our history. He was the central figure in that awful drama enacted at Goliad and, like Travis, Bowie, Crockett, and Bonham, a pathetic interest attaches to him as one of the martyrs to Texas liberty. He was a brave, dashing and noble fellow and really a true patriot. But he was too heady, too vaporing, too vacillating, for a practical military leader. His blunders in the capacity of commander not only cost his own life but the lives of hundreds of other brave and valuable men—"all fine, florid, young fellows," as their executioners referred to them. Fannin was a soldier of fortune. He gambled with fate—and lost. Had he survived the war he would no doubt have fared well at the hands of the people of Texas. From the little of a reliable nature that has come down to us concerning Fannin, it appears that his career before coming to Texas was colorful enough; and it was somewhat an unsavory one.[32]

James Walker Fannin, Jr.—the name was originally Fanning—was the natural son of a Georgia planter. A failure at West Point, where he spent eighteen months, he went back south to become a slave trader. This traffic was outlawed by the United States and all other civilized nations and those engaged in it were considered "pirates." So Fannin was *a pirate*.

His first trip to Texas was made in 1834, clearing Havana port by making the false affidavit that

---

[32] From Historian Wharton's "The Goliad Campaign" and his "Remember Goliad" we learn most that the world will perhaps ever know of this notable character, previous to his coming to Texas.

his boat carried "fourteen free negroes." On his way to Texas, whence he fled to escape his creditors, he was imprisoned for debt at New Orleans. He had a leaky pen and left promissory notes all the way from Georgia to Texas. But for all this he was so young, only thirty years; was handsome and brave, a charming personality, a devoted husband and father. But for Fannin's love for glamorous war, and its fortunes, he might have lived the peaceful, prosperous life of a planter and become a leading citizen of Texas.

In coming to Texas Fannin had ambitions other than becoming a slave trader, or a soldier of fortune. He desired to be a planter, and to that purpose, in January, 1836, he concluded the purchase of one-half interest in the fine 3000 acre plantation of Joseph Mims, on the San Bernard, for the sum of $25,000.00, paying "twenty-three African negroes valued at $17,250.00, and executing his note for $7,750.00." His wife and two little daughters had already joined him at Brazoria, and it was his purpose to settle down with his family, on the plantation, as soon as the war was over. But fate was against Fannin. His wife eventually returned to the states, where she died a few years later. The youngest of his daughters and the last of the family, bereft of reason for more than half a century, died, a ward in the State Asylum at Austin in 1896.

While his fame and fortune were high in camp, Fannin procured a furlough, November 22nd, and suddenly left for his plantation. "A week later," says Wharton, "he was busy rousing the country on the lower Brazos. Two weeks later he was named recruiting officer by the council and hurrying up and down the coast country, warrior and agitator." The council, invasion bent, over the head of cautious, practical, old Governor Smith, had issued Colonel Fannin a wide, ample, plenary commission, empowering him "to raise, collect, and concentrate all volunteer troops now at the mouth of the Brazos, Bexar, or elsewhere, who are willing to enter an expedition against Matamoros."

Armed with such authority Colonel Fannin rode hard to Velasco where two days later he issued his warlike broadcast: "To the west-face. March! The expedition to the West has been ordered by the general council and volunteers are ordered to concentrate at San Patricio on the 21st to 27th of January. The fleet will follow along the coast and we will keep the war out of Texas." Governor Smith vetoed the orders of the council authorizing the expedition to Matamoros and the loose commissions to Fannin and Johnson. The council now countered by impeaching Smith from office, Lieutenant-Governor Robinson assuming and signing himself acting-governor. Matters were now moving in a wild and confused way; and the result came near being fatal. When the volunteer companies began to arrive in Texas early in January, 1836, Fannin, as the accredited agent of the government, received and took charge of them.

The summer and autumn of 1835, were wild seasons in Texas. There were "wars and rumors of wars." Fannin came from real American patriot stock, and as the rumors of war spread, his patriotism kindled and he was ready, anxious for strife. At a banquet in Brazoria, October 8, in honor of the great Empressario Stephen Austin, just returned from his long, dreary, weary, imprisonment in the city of Mexico, Fannin was one of the guests and he responded to the beautiful toast: "Union. May the people of Texas unite roses, white and red, and their only emulation shall be who will do the most for the public good."

About this time a Mexican war vessel with a considerable force of soldiers and military supplies, anchored in Copano Bay. The troop was commanded by General Cos, a brother-in-law of Santa Anna, and sent out to garrison the important post at Bexar. Fannin conceived the vaunting scheme of organizing a rough rider brigade to dash down and intercept the Mexicans on their way to San Antonio. Failing, however, to raise a sufficient force to carry out his plan, he did head a small company called the Brazos Guards, and set forth to Gonzales, joining the patriot army and marching with it to San Antonio. The noted adventurer and author, Sealfield, then in Texas, joined Captain Fannin's company when it left the Brazos for the seat of war, and he gives a colorful account of the expedition: "We left with 34 men mounted on mustangs, each equipped with a rifle and bowie knife, powder horn and bullet bag."

With the patriot army during the month or more in the vicinity of Bexar, Fannin participated in all skirmishes and battles and was always in the thick of the fight. In the fierce engagement near Mission Conception, October 28, Fannin and James Bowie commanded, and each displayed much cool bravery. Fannin so distinguished himself as to win the popular title of "Hero of Conception." Thus Fannin began his brief military career.

The second swing of the revolution, following the brilliant affair at Bexar, during the Yuletide of 1835, was of a filibustering nature and most disastrous. The civil government of Texas was quarreling and warring—Governor Smith having been impeached. General Houston's authority as commander-in-chief was set at naught, and disaster came thick and fast. There was no united action in either civil or military affairs—the darkest days in all Texas history had come.

Meanwhile, through the efforts of Commissioners Austin, Wharton, and Archer to the States, military companies were organizing at several points in the south and were hastening toward Texas. But there was no unity of command to receive these valuable volunteers. The wild schemes hatched by the errant Doctor Grant for the capture of Matamoros were rife everywhere; and the scheme was alluring. Johnson and Grant, with their small forces, were at San Patricio, preparing to lead the raid into Mexico. Colonel Fannin with a commission from the usurping Lieutenant-Governor Robinson, recognized himself as the commander of the "Army of Invasion," with headquarters at Goliad.

The tragedy in which Colonel Fannin played the leading role began about March 2nd, the day on which Texas declared her independence, and the final page in the bloody drama was written on Palm Sunday, March 27th, 1836, while Texas was still struggling to establish that independence. But in justice to Fannin it should be stated that the unstable civil government was the cause of all the trouble; and it came near sealing the fate of Texas. Witness: After Governor Smith was deposed, acting-governor and commander-in-chief of the army, Robinson, on February 13th, issued new instructions to agent Fannin: "You will occupy such points as in your opinion you deem best. Fortify and defend Goliad and Bexar and give the enemy battle if he advances. All former orders given by General Houston or myself are countermanded, so you may do as you deem expedient."

Accordingly, the fortress was made ready for a siege. A trench was dug about the presidio, with an opening to the river for water, the old structure was strengthened at various weak points, nine heavy cannon were mounted, everything looked secure, and the stronghold was vauntingly named "Fort Defiance."

At this very juncture Santa Anna, with his formidable army, approached Bexar, and on February 24th, the siege of the Alamo began. In his dire extremity, and realizing the stressing need of men and munitions, Travis sent his appeal, begging Fannin to come with haste to his aid. "Poor, dear Fannin, who could never refuse anybody anything," did finally decide to go, and on the last day of February the whole garrison, 300 strong, with their artillery and munitions on ox carts, marched out of their fortress to join their beleaguered friends in the Alamo.

But now a fatal accident—Just after crossing the San Antonio river, and while still in view of the fort, one of the ox carts broke down, a cold winter rain was pelting down, a halt was made, a hurried council of war was held. In their hasty preparations to leave, their provisions had been overlooked, the situation was discussed and it was decided to return to the inviting fortress.

All the while the guns of Santa Anna's army thundered away at the Alamo; and General Urrea came marching on towards Goliad, leaving a trail of blood along his path.

And now the drama draws rapidly to its close. The Mexican army of invasion was fully advised of the movements of the scattered detachments of Texan troops. As historian Wharton says: "If the Texans had left Urrea to plan their activities as best suited his purpose, they could not have served him better. Scattered in little detachments, scouting about in aimless fashion, with no precaution to prevent surprise, he fell upon them, one by one."

Captain King and his little force of 23 men —sent out to rescue endangered colonists at Refugio—was intercepted on March 14th and those not killed in the engagement were shot on orders from Urrea. The tragic slaughter of these poor unfortunate fellows was almost too pathetic to relate; a Mexican officer who witnessed the execution wrote his wife: "They were all young men, the oldest not over thirty, and of fine florid complexions. When these unfortunate youths were brought to the place of their death the lamentations and the appeals they uttered to Heaven in their own language, with extended arms, kneeling, were such as might have caused the very stones to cry out with compassion." Though the stones may have been moved with the piteous pleas of these, "fine, florid, young fellows," not so the cold-blooded chief, Urrea. Let every Texan ever remember Goliad.

But this is not the only tragic episode to be recorded. The little force of about 40 men under Frank Johnson at San Patricio, was surprised and slain, only Johnson and two or three companions escaping. "It was a simple matter to ambush and slay Dr. Grant and his 33 men who were out hunting wild horses on the plains of the Nueces, on the very day the independence of Texas was declared at Washington-on-the-Brazos. One of the noble young men who fell with Grant merits mention and the grateful memory of Texas for all time.

Robert Morris, a gallant young fellow under thirty, who commanded one company of the New Orleans Grays, had so distinguished himself in the siege of Bexar, that he had been made a major. On the last day of the year, 1835, before leaving for the West to join Fannin, he wrote his brother-in-law, Dr. Vail, at Nacogdoches: "I am in a dangerous land and may be knocked off at any time. If so, I leave my lands (military bounty) to my sisters and I will leave an immortal name. I will have accomplished what I came for in having aided to win the freedom of Texas."

Many such tragic incidents and bloody episodes were now occurring almost daily especially in the Western section of the country. We can only notice two or three of these inhuman massacres. The first and most wanton is that of 73 emigrants who left New Orleans in a schooner for Copano. "They were landed (a contemporary historian wrote[33]) unarmed at that port, trusting themselves to the power of the Mexicans; but in less than two hours, they were all butchered by the soldiers in sight of the vessel. The schooner escaped to Matagorda.

The other is the fate of the notable Dr. Harrison, a son of President Harrison. He was traveling with three other American gentlemen, when they were all taken and murdered, their bodies horribly mutilated, their bowels torn out, and then left in that situation, a prey to the vultures.

It is hard to visualize the terrible situation and condition of the country at this period. The Great Runaway Scrape was in full swing, and a general alarm and dismay seized the inhabitants. On the north the Indians, incited by Santa Anna's emissaries, were becoming emboldened and carrying on forays of plundering and murdering; from the south approached the great Mexican army of invasion, to wage a war of extermination. Before such merciless

---

[33] A. A. Parker's "The Texian War," in his "Trip to the West and Texas"—Second Edition, 1836, pp. 371-373.

foes, the inhabitants fled, like clouds of dust before the storm. In their hurried flight all possessions were abandoned and left to the merciless invaders. The settlements to the south of the Brazos, were entirely broken up and the whole country became the theatre of armies, battles, murders and massacres. But let us revert to yet more tragic and bloody scenes.

The drama moves rapidly to its close. For a brief space Major Ward and his gallant hundred, scouting around Goliad, evaded the enemy but were finally captured and *spared* as "prisoners of war"— to perish in the general massacre on the following Palm Sunday.

All these sad, rapidly transpiring disasters spread a gloomy atmosphere about Fort Defiance. And this brings us to the bloodiest episode of the revolution —the battle of Coleto, or, as the Mexicans called it, Encinal del Perdado.

The "ifs" of history are markers of mistakes. Had Fannin heeded Travis' patriotic appeal, pushed on and joined that devoted little band in the Alamo, a different and more pleasing story might be written into history. A minor incident decided him. Even when General Houston sent the heady Fannin pre-emptory orders to blow up the fortress at Goliad, fall back to Victoria, and hasten part of his force to Gonzales, he still delayed. He had ideas and ambitions of his own. But when he was warned that a large and ruthless Mexican force was bearing down upon Goliad, he made haste to evacuate the place. Dismantling the fort and burying the heavy cannon he could not carry, he set out with his troops, nine or ten pieces of artillery and some rickety ox-wagons —again forgetting his provisions—over the old Spanish Trail to Victoria.

From a military viewpoint, the rash and heady commander of the "Army of the West" made many foolish and inexcusable blunders. His fatal one came when he became unduly excited, left his stronghold and supplies at Goliad, and attempted to beat a hasty retreat out across the prairies—when too late. Historian Wharton gives the sad sequel:

"On Saturday morning, March 18th, a dense fog shrouded the presidio, the river, and the hills about, and under its cover the little army of 270[34] men and boys marched out of their fortress. There were nine cannon and a wagon filled with ammunition, three or four baggage wagons, and several carts, all drawn by oxen. It took two hours to get across the river. The men waded into the water waist deep and pulled and pushed with the tired animals."

Once across the river the force was placed in marching order and groped along through the fog, noiseless except the creaking of the wagons and the carts. It was indeed a "ghastly, gloomy, scene." From here the gallant Captain Albert Horton was detailed, with a troop of 36 men, to reconnoiter and scour the country along the route for the approaching enemy. The scouts were soon cut off, prevented from reporting, and barely escaped capture. Three men had also been detailed to ride in the rear, to give the alarm if any Mexicans approached from that direction. While the army was halting around the broken-down ammunition wagon this rear guard dashed up, yelling at the top of their voices, "The Mexicans are coming." One, a German Jew, seventeen years old, named Herman Ehrenberg, dismounted and remained to fight with his comrades. He was made prisoner and marched out to be slaughtered, but effected his escape. The other two men, under whip and spur continued their wild flight—but if they did escape, they never dared reveal their names or tell of their inglorious flight.

(34) Other writers give Fannin's force as more than three hundred men.

TALL MEN WITH LONG RIFLES

Thus the army pushed along with increased efforts, across the Manahuila Creek, and out on the Llano del Perdido, hoping to reach the Colito, with its water and sheltering timbers, for their camp. But fate was stalking close. While yet about a mile from the creek the ammunition wagon broke down. The fog was now lifting and a sight was revealed that might chill the bravest—the little force was being surrounded by large forces of the enemy. As the shrill blasts of the enemy bugles pealed across the plain, the Mexicans dashed up in battle array on all sides. The Texans made hasty preparations for defense. Massing the wagons in the center, the men were formed in a hollow square three lines deep, with artillery planted at the corners. Colonel Urrea prepared for action at once, his cavalry well to the front, supported by their large infantry forces, in the rear. In this way the battle opened, the Mexicans making simultaneous and fierce charges on all sides of the American square; and from mid-afternoon until deep into darkness, raged one of the fiercest and bloodiest engagements of the Texas Revolution.

Undismayed, and coolly, Fannin passed among his men, giving orders, cautioning them to withhold their fire until the enemy was close enough to make every shot count; and, considering that they were for the first time under fire, they behaved with the gallantry and coolness of veterans. Soon the firing became general and rapid on all sides and at close quarters. Several times the enemy in overwhelming force dashed down upon the dauntless little band and attempted a bayonet charge, but they were as often driven back by a withering fire from the American rifles. Urrea now became desperate and determined to ride down the little army in a furious headlong cavalry charge, but his men and horses were swept down by artillery fire and rifle bullets, causing the whole enemy force to retire in confusion. An eyewitness, describing the fiery onslaught, says, "The scene was now dreadful to behold; ***the wounded were rending the air with their distressing moans; while a number of horses without riders were rushing to and fro upon the enemy's lines, increasing the confusion among them; their retreat resembled the headlong flight of a herd of buffaloes rather than the retreat of a well-drilled regular army."

It was well for the Texans that the day was drawing to a close. With rapid continuous fire, the cannon had become too hot to reload, and with no water to sponge them out, were of little further use.

At sunset the main body of the enemy withdrew; but under cover of darkness trained Indian sharpshooters crawled up through the tall grass and kept up a desultory and telling fire upon the Texans—till the darkness became sufficient to reveal their exact positions from the flash of their guns, when they were silenced by the deadly aim of the American marksmen.

The dark and chilly night that followed was one of deep gloom in the disspirited Texan camp. Several of their comrades lay stark in death and sixty odd were wounded. They had no water and no provisions. However, they toiled heroically throughout the intensely dark night to strengthen their entrenchments with barricades formed mostly with the carcasses of their dead animals. Around them in every direction red camp fires of the enemy gleamed, while the bugle signals rang out at regular, short, intervals upon the chilly night air all along the cordon of sentinels that encircled and kept vigilant watch over the little band of discomfited and doomed Texans.

Meanwhile the enemy had received considerable reinforcements, a fresh supply of ammunition and two pieces of artillery, and at dawn they renewed the attack with deadlier effect. The crisis had come. Outnumbered more than seven to one, there was no hope of winning the unequal struggle, and it was useless to attempt to beat a retreat through the massed ranks of the enemy. Surrender was their only alternative. It was death, perhaps, either way. Once prisoners, by some turn in the scale of fate, they might be spared life. And, so for once, these gallant Americans raised the white flag; though it was said that Fannin at first opposed giving up, saying, "We whipped them yesterday and we can do it again today." As the unfortunate young fellows stacked their arms and filed into line as prisoners many shed tears—they had gambled with fate—and lost.

Not all the volunteers from the states who fought in the Texas Revolution were reckless adventurers, as some writers have said. Most of them were noble and patriotic, all of them heroic.

CHAPTER XVII

Fannin Gambles With Fate—And Loses

The cards of fate were now shuffled fast for the final play in the game. As customary with Mexicans, the disarmed prisoners were segregated into small groups and marched back under heavy guard to Goliad. That was a sad Sunday for those unfortunate men; but they were buoyed with sweet hope of life and liberty. Another, succeeding, sad Sunday came—that memorable Palm Sunday, March 27th, 1836.

"It was a dreary and awful week for the prisoners," says Wharton, "huddled in the Presidio chapel and guarded within the walls of the Fort Defiance they had so lately fortified with so much enthusiasm. The wounded languished and many of them died. The three surgeons, Shackleford, Bernard, and Fields, and the medical student Stevenson, were busy day and night with the wounded Mexicans and had little time for their own countrymen. Some one stole Dr. Bernard's case of instruments.

"It was the week of the full moon and these four hundred homesick young warriors watched its rise each evening over the desolate walls of the presidio and saw the long sinister shadow of the chapel tower as it moved steadily as though hiding from the bright clear face of the March moon.

"From without the dismal walls could be heard the music from a flute, the strum of a banjo, and the singing of 'Home Sweet Home' in melancholy strain—It was but the funeral dirge of these poor doomed fellows. They were never to see their earthly homes nor their loved ones again in this world.

"That Palm Sunday was a bright crisp day, but it marks the date of the darkest, most horrible, and bloodiest deed, in all Texas history. On that memorable day, 390 gallant but helpless young men were marched out in squads and shot down like dogs. Nearly all of these unfortunate men were volunteers from the States, who had so nobly responded to help the Texas cause. Among those who perished were the noble young fellows composing the New Orleans Grays, under Captain Pettes; the Mustangs of Kentucky, under Captain Duval; the Red Rovers, from Alabama, under Captain (Doctor) Shackleford; a company from Louisville, Kentucky, and one from Huntsville, Tennessee, under Captain Bradford; Captain King's company, from Georgia, and Ward's battalion. The doctors of the force and a few non-combatants were spared. At daylight on the morning of the wholesale execution, the doctors were called up and placed in a hospital outside the fort. They were not, of course, informed of the dreadful fate soon to befall their comrades.

"It appears that the doomed men were marched out of the fort in four divisions; one on the Bexar road, one on the Corpus Christi road, and two towards the lower ford, some half to three-fourths of a mile, guarded by soldiers on either side. It seems the prisoners were told different stories; that they were to go for wood; to drive up beeves; to proceed to Corpus, etc., and so little suspicion had they of the awful fate awaiting them that it was not until the guns were leveled at their breasts that they were aroused to a sense of their situation. Suddenly they were halted, one file of the guards quickly passed through the ranks of the prisoners to the other side and ordered the prisoners to sit down with their backs to the guards. Instantly young Fenner rose to his feet and exclaimed, *'Boys they are going to kill us—die with your faces to them, like men!'* At the same time, two other young men, flourishing

THE MASSACRE AT GOLIAD

their caps over their heads, shouted at the top of their voices, 'Hurrah for Texas!' Instantly and altogether, the firing began."

One of the most graphic accounts of the horrible butchery was written by the private secretary of Major Miller, then a lad of 18 years of age, and who witnessed the whole scene,[35] he says:

"The morning of the massacre was slightly foggy. Without understanding wherefore, we of Miller's command, were ordered to tie a *white* band around our left arms; some of us tore pieces from our shirts for that purpose. This was to distinguish us from Fannin's men, who alone were doomed. We were conducted out to a peach and fig grove, in front of the church, and in sight of two of the three parties into which Fannin's men were divided; the third being out of view behind the church, near the river bank. When the firing began, boy as I was, I was impressed by the varied expressions in the faces of our men, thus made unexpected witnesses of the awful tragedy. Surprise, horror, grief and revenge were depicted in the most vivid lines. At first all were startled; some became at once horror stricken; others wept in silent agony; still others laughed in their passion, swore, clinched their teeth, and looked like demons. Now, at the lapse of more than a quarter of a century, I can never think or talk of that dreadful scene with any degree of composure. Some of the poor fellows attempted to escape, and of course outrun the Mexicans; but then the cavalry! Just as one of these men of Fannin's had gotten fairly clear of his pursuers, a mounted Mexican from close by me at once started on the chase, and catch-

[35] This narrative was written by Major Miller's private, who signed himself S. H. B. and was first published in Barber and Howes History of the United States, in 1861. See pp. 1358-59. For many years Mr. S. H. B.................was a well known merchant of Cincinnati. Will some one who may know the name of Major Miller's private secretary, kindly supply the full name.

ing up with him, cut him down. Never did I so want to hamstring a horse. Those not killed outright, were deliberately butchered by the Mexicans, men and women, and stripped. This over, some of them, even the women, as they passed us by on their returned ladened with plunder, insulted us by the grossest vulgarities, shook their fists in our faces, swearing in taunting tones and the vilest words—'Your turn—to-morrow!'

"In about an hour more, the wounded left in the barracks were dragged out into the fort yard and butchered. Colonel Fannin was the last victim. When informed of his fate, he met it like a soldier. He handed his watch to the officer whose business it was to murder him, and requested that he be shot in the *breast* and not in the *head,* and likewise to see that his remains should be decently buried. With that perfidy which is so prominent a characteristic of the Mexican race, all requests were ignored. Fannin seated himself in a chair, tied the handkerchief over his eyes, and bared his bosom to receive the fire of the soldiers.

"The stripped bodies of the slain were collected and placed in piles. Those of the wounded who had been massacred at the fort, Fannin among the rest were chucked stark naked into carts, like so many dead hogs, carried out and dumped on top of the others. Brush was then piled over the whole and set on fire. It took several days successive burnings to consume them. Nightly the prairie wolves gathered to feast on the half roasted bodies, and kept up their howlings through all the long hours, and as the day dawned their execrable screams increased, in rage at being thus driven by the morning light from their horrid banquet."

April, rich with fragrance of bud and bloom, passed away with little incident at Goliad. But the blood of the martyred heroes was calling from the stained earth for revenge. Now and then a courier from some division of the invading army, now far to the east, came riding hard with dispatches on his way to Mexico.

Then came a rumor of San Jacinto and in the first days of May it was confirmed by a fugitive horseman who had outrun his fellows in the flight.

Soon General Urrea passed through Goliad—in headlong flight, urging everybody to flee to the border. A little later, May 14th, Filisola, with a ragged remnant of the mighty army which had reached Texas in February with banners flying, reached the town and halted a short time; but even this brave soldier could not long endure a stay in the dreary, uncanny place, and on May 25th, 1836, horse, foot, and dragoon, bag and baggage, the Mexican army left Goliad forever.

And now the most tragic and most pathetic episode of the history of Texas draws to a close. A month after the terrible slaughter of their comrades at Goliad, Drs. Bernard and Shackleford again rode into the deserted town. They did not tarry in the desolate place, but hastened on out to the field of Coleto, where they had witnessed disaster. Here they paused, says Wharton, and viewed the scattered bones of their comrades, including Shackleford's son and nephew, who had fallen there, and while yet contemplating the scene they saw an army approaching across the plain, and at its head rode General Rusk.

On Friday morning, June 3rd, there was an imposing funeral near the old presidio. The remains of the murdered men had been gathered and a huge grave dug. The Texas army was paraded and Colonel Sidney Sherman lead the march. Five mourners, men then with the army and who had escaped the massacre, walked before General Rusk and his staff. A minute gun was fired from the walls as the procession moved, and at the grave the soldier-orator, Rusk, pronounced a funeral oration.

Here the tragic story of Fannin and his men closes, even identity of their last resting place was long lost. But the memory of these noble martyrs to Texan liberty was not neglected; and after a lapse of more than half a century—thanks to the untiring efforts of Lou W. Kemp and a few other patriotic Texans, the grave of these men has recently (May, 1934) been definitely located and will be permanently marked.

Soon after the battle of San Jacinto, General Rusk, the new commander of the Texan army, ordered a military funeral for Fannin and his men. The order read that "the skeletons and bones of our murdered brethren be collected in one place in front of the fort and buried with all the honors of war.'

As a part of the ceremonies instructions were issued to Major Geo. W. Poe to have "a minute gun fired from the fort commencing with the time the procession moves until it arrives at the grave." Thus the sad rites were duly performed and the "place of sepulchre was marked with a large pile of rocks."

Time passed. Those who knew of the burial place had died, even the very plot had been put into a farm, the loose rocks marking the sacred spot had been carted away and all traces of the grave obliterated.

Our historians have confused themselves through General Rusk's burial order, and in concluding that the burial took place in front of the fort. The long overlooked instructions to Major Poe to fire a minute gun from the time the procession moved until it arrived at the grave, put a different aspect on the matter. From this it was clear that the bones were conveyed to the fort, then buried elsewhere—but where? Oldest settlers of that section were interviewed, old maps and town plats gave no light on the quesion. The enterprising J. de Cordova, in his valuable little book published in 1858 and now long out of print, refers to the military burial of the Fannin men; and says the grave was "marked with a pile of rocks." But no rock pile was to be found in the vicinity—the rocks had been carted off and placed along the fence hedges when the land about had been put in cultivation.

From time to time the search continued, but in vain—until assistance came through the tell-tale work of a colony of gophers. The burroughing rodents had selected a domicile on the peak of a hill across the ravine from the fort, and in their "diggings" had unearthed some small, partly charred bones. That was an important find. Dr. J. E. Pearce, professor of anthropology at the University of Texas, was called to make excavations; and his researches soon established the fact that the grave of these martyr-heroes was definitely located.

Historian Kemp calls this "the most important discovery made in Texas during the years that I have been interested in this sort of work."

A beautiful drive from the projected Austin-Refugio highway to the grave site, a distance of some fifteen hundred feet, has already been planned and a movement is being launched to have the state provide a suitable monument and develop a park shrine.

The discovery of the long lost and neglected burial place of Fannin and his men gives added interest to the much discussed question of how they surrendered — *conditional* or *unconditional*. The matter yet remains open for controversy by historical writers. What we shall say will hardly settle the matter. When historians disagree, let the reader make his own history.

There has been much discussion as to the terms of this surrender and the matter is still involved in some uncertainty. Dr. Shackleford, the faithful historian of Fannin's command, as well as the other few survivors of the massacre, always stoutly contended that the articles of surrender were written in both English and Spanish, were signed and carefully read over in the presence of many of the troops and that they specifically provided that the Americans should be treated as prisoners of war and should be returned to the States at once. General Urrea and all the other Mexican officials have stoutly maintained that the surrender was *unconditional*.

In the archives of the War Department in the City of Mexico, may be seen the documents claimed to be the originals of Fannin's capitulation on the battle field of Coleto. These documents were recently (1910) read, and photostatic copies made by Dr. Eugene C. Barker, head of the Department of History, University of Texas. With Dr. Barker's permission we give a true translation of the instrument:

"*Surrender of the forces found at Goliad.*

Article 1. *Under orders of James W. Fannin— The Mexican troops having been posted with their battery one hundred and sixty paces and having opened fire, we raised a white flag. Immediately Captain D. Juan Morales and D. Mariano Salas, accompanied by Lieutenant-Colonel of the Engineers, Don Juan Jose Holzinger, came immediately. We proposed to surrender at discretion on such terms as they deemed proper.*

Article 2. That the wounded and Comandante Fannin be treated with all consideration, on the condition that they deliver up their arms.

Article 3. That all the detachments be treated as prisoners of war and placed at the disposition of the Supreme Government.

Campo on Coleto between the Guadalupe and La Bahia, March 20, 1836.

J. M. Chadwick,
B. C. Wallace, Major

Approved, J. W. Fannin, Commander

Attached to this instrument is a postscript, signed by General Urrea, which reads: "Since, when the white flag was raised by the enemy I made it known to their officer that I could not grant any other terms than an unconditional surrender and they agreed to it through the officers expressed, those who subscribe the surrender have no right to any other terms. They have been informed of this fact and they are agreed. I ought not, cannot, nor wish to grant any other terms.—Jose Urrea.

This is a copy, Mexico, March 7, 1837.

Ignacio del Corral."

It is noticable that the only Mexican signature to the document is that of Urrea, which follows the addendum written in his language and—as historian Wharton says—probably in his own handwriting, below the signatures of Chadwick, Wallace, and Fannin.

"A careful study of article 1 (the Preamble," says Wharton, "and Urrea's addendum leaves a very distinct impression that they were both written after the surrender.

"Our good first historian, Henderson Yoakum, when gathering data for his great 'History of Texas' nearly three-quarters of a century ago, had access to this document and denounced it as a forgery. It has always been believed in Texas and has much appearance of truth, that the postscript added to this document and bearing the signature of Urrea was written after he and Santa Anna returned to Mexico.[36]"

Referring particularly to the terms and conditions of the surrender, Dr. Shackleford says that Fannin was loath to give up, saying, "We whipped them yesterday, and we can whip them again today." To this the doctor remarked to Fannin that he would not oppose a surrender "provided we could obtain an *honorable capitulation,* one on which we could rely, and that if he could not obtain such, come back; our graves are already dug, let us all be buried together." To these remarks the men responded in a firm and determined manner, and the colonel assured us that he would never surrender on any other terms.

The doctor was a man of high character, very cool, careful and deliberate, and he gives the terms of the surrender as he and the Americans well understood them, and on the conditions upon which they laid down their arms. These terms are very much at variance with those exhibited by the Mexicans. Dr. Shackleford gives the terms of surrender as follows:

"1. That the Texans should be received and treated as prisoners of war, according to the usages of civilized nations.

---

(36) Wharton's "Remember Goliad."

"2. That private property should be respected and restored; but that the side arms of the officers must be given up.

"3. That the men should be sent to Copano, and thence, in eight days, to the United States, or as soon thereafter as vessels could be procured to take them.

"4. That the officers should be paroled and returned to the United States in like manner."

Another thing goes to substantiate the fact that the prisoners were promised freedom and quick return home. On Thursday, following the surrender, Fannin, though suffering with a severe wound, rode with Colonel Holzinger of the Mexican army to Copano to arrange for a boat. But no boat was there and they returned to Goliad Saturday.

The massacre of these noble men brought down upon Santa Anna and Urrea the condemnation of the civilized world. The flimsy excuse of Santa Anna for ordering them shot, and the promptness of Urrea in having the order carried out, was that these men were *foreigners*—pirates—that they had invaded Mexico and were fighting under a "strange, unknown flag."

When the Mexican army set out from San Luis Potosi on its march for Texas, General Santa Anna issued (December 7, 1835) certain orders to his generals, by which they should be governed during the campaign. One paragraph of this order read:

"These foreigners who are making war against the Mexican Nation are in violation of all laws and are not to be accorded any consideration whatever, and for this reason you will not give them quarter, and you will so order your troops at your first opportunity. These foreigners having audaciously declared war to the death against Mexicans should be dealt with accordingly."

This was the fallen Mexican chief's excuse, at

San Jacinto, for the dastardly, cold-blooded butchery at Goliad.

Thus the drama drew to its close and the curtain came down on this bloody scene. It was a terrible loss of noble young men; but the sacrifice of these martyrs to Texan liberty was not in vain. Their blood called out from the plains of Goliad and retributive justice came swift and sure on the field of San Jacinto.—What price liberty!

It will be remembered that when Fannin set forth on his retreat he sent Captain Horton, with his little cavalry company, in advance to examine the crossing on the Coleto and to watch for the approach of the Mexicans. While at the stream he suddenly found himself surrounded by Urrea's army and barely escaped capture. Unable to join his chief he dashed away to Victoria, hoping to secure reinforcements; but Commander Dimmit had already left that post in flight toward the Colorado. "Horton," says Shackleford, "should not be censured; he had done all in his power to relieve his companions, and an attempt to reach the battle ground would almost inevitably have resulted in death or captivity of the whole party." Thus Horton and his troop of 36 men escaped the massacre.

I knew a few of the men who escaped the slaughter at Goliad, and have heard them tell the story of their miraculous escapes—John C. Duval, William B. Hunter, and Dillard Cooper.

Duval was a man of much literary ability, and he wrote and published a very interesting narrative of that horrible affair. The work is a classic in Texas history.

Hunter was a young lawyer who had quit a lucrative practice and joined the New Orleans Grays. His escape from death in the massacre is one of the most miraculous on record. At the first fire he fell-

pierced by a ball, and a Mexican soldier, to make sure of his demise cut his throat, and to make doubly sure, thrust him with a bayonet and beat him over the head with the butt of his musket. He then stripped Hunter of his clothing and left him where he had fallen. Here the poor fellow lay until nightfall, when he dragged himself to the river and managed to cross over and, in agonizing pain, crawled on for some miles, finally wandering into a Mexican ranch. A kind Mexican woman concealed him in a thick brush, and for a week she came to him regularly at night with food and water. When he was able to travel she clothed him in some old Mexican garments, provided him with food, and he trudged on for days until he finally reached the Texan army.

After the war Hunter returned to Goliad, where he lived and practiced his profession. Years later he was a senator in the legislature of Texas; while Dr. Barnhard served as representative in the lower house, from Goliad. Many visited these two notable survivors to listen to their stories of the horrible massacre, and they loved to keep the memory of their slain comrades fresh in the hearts of the people.

Dillard Cooper was probably the last survivor of the massacre. He died in extreme poverty at Llano, Texas, in the early nineties. During his latter years the pitiful pension of $150.00 a year, provided by the great and opulent state of Texas, barely sufficed to buy food and medicines for the aged hero and his faithful wife. Napoleon was not far wrong when he said, "Republics are ungrateful."

One other and most unique character escaped death on that terrible occasion. The serio-comic story of this fellow's escape is told by Creed Taylor:

"I personally knew most of the men who escaped at Goliad, and have often listened to their recitals of that bloody affair. One of the most interesting being the escape of a young man, called 'Kentuck.' This fine young fellow was one of the volunteers from Kentucky; but of his past I knew nothing, nor did he impart his real name, being known to the boys in the camp only by the nick-name of 'Kentuck.' He was a man of small stature, rather handsome of features, and probably 22 or 23 years old. He was a jolly good fellow and fairly well educated. Many old Texans will remember this unique and somewhat noted character of the early days of Texas. I can vouch for the truth of his story.

"To enable the reader to appreciate the terrible ordeal to which Kentuck was subjected on that occasion, it is important to describe his wardrobe. All except his underwear was thick and heavy, consisting of jeans, pants and vest, a blanket overcoat and rawhide boots. From his guards he learned the Mexican game of monte, in which he soon excelled his teachers. He won about 300 silver dollars, the total weight of which was about eighteen pounds; and for the lack of a bag in which to carry this money, he had distributed it in the several pockets of his garments.

"On the night of the 26th of March, the prisoners were told that on the next day they were to be shipped from Copano Bay to New Orleans; and on the following morning, Palm Sunday, they were marched out single file, between two files of guards, and in separate divisions; two squads to the river bank, and one a few hundred yards east—ostensibly for marching to the coast.

"'Kentuck' was in one of the divisions marched to the river bank. They were made to form single file a few feet from the rivers brink, and the Mexican file next to the river passed through them to the other side. Now the guards, outnumbering them two to one, were all on one side, and the prisoners naturally turned and faced them. The enemy's purpose could no longer be concealed. Instantly the prisoners became aware that they were to be shot, and poor, emaciated, half starved fellows, they were powerless to resist; else they might have rushed upon the file of soldiers, disarmed them and escaped, as did the Mier men at Hacienda Salado in 1842.

"At that moment they heard the firing upon the other squads and the terrible screams of the wounded and dying men. 'Kentuck' and his comrades were ordered to 'face about'—turn their backs to their guards—but many of them, including 'Kentuck,' scorned the order, and continued to look straight into the eyes of their murderers. When the order was given to 'Fire,' many of the firing squad appeared to be more nervous than their unfortunate victims. Some of the Mexicans had not the courage to shoot brave men who could look into their eyes in the moment of death; and the man who faced 'Kentuck' did not fire, though nearly all others were killed.

"As his slain comrades fell, 'Kentuck' also fell—back into the river. He tried to swim across the stream, but encumbered by his heavy garments and his pockets loaded with silver, he made poor headway. The current bore him downstream and held him long enough to saturate his garments and fill his boots with water, and he came near drowning. Finally he reached the opposite bank, climbed up, and ran for his life. His heavy garments weighed him down, the heavy silver in his pockets beat upon him, and the sloshing water in his boots caused his feet to slide within them. Thus impeded and excited he thought he was scarcely moving.

"Looking back over his shoulder he saw some of the Mexicans were pursuing him. They could not bring their muskets to bear on him as they swam across the river, but he could hear their swords clanking. Gradually they gained upon him, but when almost near enough to strike him, as luck would have it, in twisting about trying to elude them, some money jostled out of his pocket, and his pursuers halted and scuffled for the coins. This enabled 'Kentuck' to gain considerable distance and it gave him an idea. As his pursuers again drew near, he threw down a handful of money, for which they again halted and scuffled. Thus handful after handful of his dollars went until all of his pockets were empty. He threw off his overcoat, which greatly lightened his burden; and then his vest, his pursuers stopping and scuffling for each of these. His hard running in the wet rawhide boots had stretched them, so that he managed to kick them off, and thereby caused his pursuers another delay and scuffle.

"'Kentuck' said that he did not mind the loss of his money and his garments so much, but he soon realized the importance of the loss of his boots. The prairie grass had recently been burned and the sharp stubble penetrated his socks and pierced his feet, causing great pain; but he was runnning for his life and did not relax his speed. His pants were burdensome and he dropped them; but, being wet, they did not slip easily from his extremities, causing him to tangle up and fall; but he did not halt, rolling over and over until he freed himself, then bounding on again with renewed effort. He had no more 'graft' with which to bribe his pursuers, and as they gained on him, 'Kentuck' said he thought that at last he was 'a gone coon skin;' but just then he reached a dense chaparral thicket into which he plunged and hid from his pursuers who beat around for a while and then gave up the pursuit.

"After a short breathing spell, 'Kentuck' pushed on, making his way in great pain through the thorny chaparral and prickly pears. His under garments were reduced to shreds and his flesh fearfully torn. In this plight he dragged himself on, and emerged into the open again, fell in with a comrade who had also feigned death, and escaped from the slaughter.

"These comrades hurried on, avoiding roads as far as possible for fear of being overtaken by some party of the enemy. All families on their route had fled eastward, but they found plenty of food in the abandoned homes. Striking the trail of Houston's army at the crossing of the San Bernard, they hurried on, arriving at the Texan camp at Foster's Plantation on the last day of March: a wonderful trial of speed on foot, from Goliad to the Brazos in four days and nights.

"Upon reaching the army 'Kentuck' and his comrade were in fearful plight; but the boys soon togged them up and, after their wounds and sores were treated, and with a little rest and sleep, they were ready for duty. They joined Houston's forces and both fought gallantly at San Jacinto. I remember seeing 'Kentuck' the next day after the battle, and he was very much interested in a game of monte. I have often heard the story of his thrilling escape and flight, substantially as I have above narrated. Of the subsequent career of 'Kentuck' I know nothing, and I regret that I did not learn his real name and more of his history."

Of Fannin's gesture in and about Goliad and of the massacre, Creed Taylor, of course, had no personal knowledge; but from frequent conversations with the few survivors, he was convinced that the accounts given by Yoakum and other early historians, are in the main correct. All testimony proves the fact that Colonel Fannin was a brave man, but as a commander he was a failure. He could and should have joined forces with Travis at San Antonio; or, as a final measure, he could have retreated from

Goliad before it was too late. "Fannin," says Taylor, "really sacrificed his men. He knew that a large Mexican army was approaching from the direction of Matamoros; that Grant's men had been captured and slain; and that San Patricio had been invested. Yet, with all this knowledge and warning, he delayed and allowed the ruthless enemy to reach Refugio and destroy the garrison stationed there; and when the glint of the foes' guns could be seen from the walls of La Bahia, he gathered his faithful followers about him and in confusion and disorder began his futile and fatal retreat. But alas! Too late. The darkest episode in Texas history was soon enacted."

CHAPTER XVIII

The Greatest Day in Texas History

The most glorious and far-reaching event in Texas history is the battle of San Jacinto—one of the shortest, sharpest, and most decisive battles of the world. One historian calls it: "Fifteen Minutes of Destiny," and so it was. The word, "jacinto," is the Spanish word for hyacinth; and it is strange that in seeking for an emblematic flower the patriotic Texan women of a later time did not choose that blossom as the one and only fitting symbol of heroic Texas.

The battle of San Jacinto has been, by men who never venture beyond the surface of thought, spoken of in terms of derision and contempt. They have measured its dignity and importance by the numbers engaged and the casualties of the conflict, but the philosophic student of history does not measure the imporance of battles by such standards. Judged in its true light, history attests that San Jacinto was the most important and most decisive military engagement which has been fought on this continent since Cornwallis surrendered on the plains of Yorktown.

One feature of the battle of San Jacinto has never been stressed to the extent it deserves: Taking the battles of the world and averaging the casualties, it will be found that the proportion of wounded to killed is about three or four to one, and many great battles have lasted all day, and even for two or three days, thus reversing the usual proportion. There is no precedent for such fatality as resulted at San Jacinto, in all the records of history. That undisciplined, ununiformed little army of frontiersmen set a standard of deadly battle which remains as yet without a parallel in the annals of history.

Every school child in Texas, and in all America, knows something about San Jacinto and Sam Houston. Many graphic accounts of the great battle have been written. Orators on patriotic Texas themes always reach their climax with the great victory, poets have sung of its valorous deeds, and artists have attempted to paint its dramatic scenes. The most intimate accounts of this extraordinary affair have come to us from actual participants and eyewitnesses. Few of the early Texan soldiers, however, were men of letters—they were fighters, more adept with the rifle than with the pen. For one thing, every soldier regarded the occasion of that day as a most serious one. The author has conversed with scores of San Jacinto men, and not one ever spoke jestingly of the incidents of that engagement—all felt that it was to be a struggle in which they would win or die. One of the most intimate and illuminating narratives that has come down to us is that of the noted old Texas soldier, Creed Taylor, who gives a vivid picture of incidents occurring on that eventful day of April 21, 1836. He says:

"The morning of April 21st dawned bright and crisp. It was to be a great day for Texas. From their crude pallets the boys sprang up as if for a joyous holiday. Merry jests went the rounds, and the camp wits spared neither high private nor officers. 'If you get bumped off, Bill, won't you will me your coonskin cap?' Tomlinson said to a comrade: 'You can take the cap now; I'll wear a Mexican officer's hat on parade tomorrow,' rejoined the confident comrade. And he was as good as his word, for he did wear a dead Mexican officer's uniform the next day.

"The night preceding the battle was a restless one to many of the boys, but General Houston slept soundly, as if nothing out of the ordinary was to take place on the morrow. As the first beams of the morning sun touched his eyelids, he rose from his blanket, walked to the bay nearby and bathed his face. At the moment a raven was seen flying across the field from the direction of the Mexican camp—interpreted by Houston as a good omen, heralding the dawn of the natal day of free Texas.

"The day was to be a memorable one in the history of Texas and a most eventful one in the life of Sam Houston. More than 20 years before as a young ensign, Houston led his men over the breastworks of a savage foe at Tohopeka—to win his first laurels as a soldier, but at the cost of severe wounds. Today he would lead his men over the breastworks of another equally bloodthirsty enemy, to win great military renown and added wounds.

"As the forenoon wore away the hilarity subsided, giving place to anxiety and impatience. The boys expected to be led into battle at an early hour. Why this delay? Ten o'clock, eleven o'clock, twelve o'clock came, and no forward movement. During the noon hour, however, a number of officers approached General Houston, where he was reclining under a tree. I was not close enough to hear what was said, but observed by their gestures that some of them were intensely excited. I saw Houston rise up and with vehement motions of his clinched fists, address the party. Pretty soon the leather-faced old scout, Deaf Smith, with Jim Reeves, Mose Lapham, and one or two others, rode up to the general's headquarters, and after a short conversation dashed away at full speed. No one knew their orders or destination, but all knew that something was going to happen soon and the excitement was at high pitch.

"And here is opportunity to correct another error that has crept into history—to the effect that General Houston suggested the destruction of Vince's Bridge.

TALL MEN WITH LONG RIFLES

That idea was first advanced by John Coker, a private in the cavalry corps; and in this way. As he was talking with a group of his comrades about reinforcements reaching the enemy he remarked that the destruction of the bridge over Vince's Bayou, some eight miles west of camp, would halt their advance. All agreed that the idea was a wise one, and Deaf Smith was requested to place the matter before General Houston. The general thought the suggestion a good one and ordered Smith to select a few trusty helpers, evade the enemy, and proceed at once to the crossing and destroy the bridge. The structure was not chopped down, as stated by some of our historians but was fired and burned away. A larger force would have been required to cut down the massive and lengthy structure in so short a time. Santa Anna himself states that in his attempt to escape, his flight was halted when he found the bridge over the bayou was burned. Private John Coker should have credit for suggesting the burning of Vince's bridge.

"As Scout Smith and his little party dashed away the excitement increased. As the boys began to gather about headquarters, the general mounted his horse which stood saddled nearby, and made a short speech, telling them to prepare to fight; that they were brave soldiers and would win the battle and 'all would be captains'; that the enemy was hemmed in and could not escape or receive reinforcements—Vince's Bridge was being destroyed—but that it would take some tall fighting to whip them. 'Remember my boys, (a favorite expression with the general) you are fighting for Texas and your loved ones, to avenge the inhuman butchery of your friends and comrades at the Alamo and at Goliad![37] The spirits of these

---

(37) "Much controversy, it appears, has arisen as to how the battle-cry "Remember the Alamo! Remember Goliad!" came about. The first time I remember to have heard these expressions was during Houston's short talk to the men on the eve of the battle. Of course the boys were continually talking about the butchery at the Alamo and the slaughter at Goliad; and avowing to avenge the

brave men call to us for revenge. Remember your wives and little children who are now in flight to escape the fury of the ruthless invaders; the red-handed war lord, Santa Anna, having boasted he would pursue and annihilate the rebel Texans and then wash his hands of their blood in the Sabine. The time and the situation is here and we will win if everyones does his duty. We must win or die. Let us fight fast and hard.' This was the trend of the talk the General made as he rode among us with uplifted sword frequently pointing towards the enemy's camp, and it certainly inspired and nerved everyone to a high pitch, and everyone was ready and anxious for the struggle.

"Going into battle of course carries serious feelings for most men; but I know I was not scared. I thought only of fighting, and I believe every man was anxious for the fray. Somehow I felt that we would win. When our line was formed and just before the order to advance was given, I looked up and down the ranks to see if anyone looked scared. The boys had remarked about the nervous state of mind of some of the officers and some believed them unduly excited. As I looked into the faces of these men I could see no signs of uneasiness. On the contrary, there was a spirit of cheerfulness, and levity that was remarkable under such conditions. Captain

---

cold blooded murder of their countrymen. But the manner in which the expression became the battle-cry at San Jacinto has never been given in a published history. The honor of coining the slogan belongs to Wm. F. Young, who fought as a private in Lamar's cavalry corps; and in this way: As the Texans charged and the Mexicans fired their first and most effective volley, killing three Amercans and wounding several, the undisciplined Texan force seemed to waver for a moment; and it was at this critical juncture that private Young dashed forward, crying at the top of his voice, 'Boys, come on! Remember the Alamo! Remember Goliad.' At once the cry was taken up and spread from man to man until the whole force was crying 'Remember the Alamo! Remember Goliad!' and it certainly carried consternation to the ranks of the Mexicans, many of them throwing down their guns, and crying out, 'Me no Alamo! Me no Goliad!' Young was severely wounded but continued to fight until the battle was over.

"The heroic man who coined and actually gave impetus to the slogan which no doubt went far toward winning the fight at San Jacinto, was one of the volunteers from South Carolina. He sleeps on Texas soil, his grave neglected. The state should honor and perpetuate his memory with a monument of lasting bronze."

Karnes did not dismount and walk excitedly back and forth before his company as has been reported. He sat during the few minutes we remained in line on his horse directly in front of us and replied in his own dry, droll way to the jests of his men in the ranks.

"The order was then given by the company leaders to 'arm and line.' As the different companies formed and were drawn up they were briefly addressed by their respective captains. I remember hearing Mosley Baker as he harangued his men in loud, unmistakable terms. The speech attracted the attention of General Houston as he rode up and down the lines, and he halted and sat quietly on his horse, listening interestedly and approvingly. Captain Baker told his men neither to ask for nor to give quarter; that now was the chance to even up the scores and avenge the murder of their comrades at San Antonio and Goliad; and as a reminder he proposed that the company carry a red flag. This met with approval and a large red handkerchief was hoisted on a pole and carried into battle.

"Engrossed in the movements of my own company, I noticed but little of the formation and movements of the other bodies of troops, except those under Colonel Ed Burleson, which took place in front of our camp. They stood rank and file two deep, and I well remember seeing the Colonel mounted on a large bay horse, riding up and down in front of the line as he addressed his men. But evidently he did not need to encourage them, for they seemed only too eager for action—swaying forward and out of line at points where the under officers were not holding them back by the flat part of their swords.

"Once again I noticed Colonel Burleson—just before the yell was raised to charge, and as he galloped over for some purpose to Sherman's line. As he dashed back across the plain, his blue flannel shirt fluttering in the breeze and his sword glistening in the sun, the spectacle was truly inspiring and we could not help cheering him. He was the picture of a real military hero. All, of course, noticed Colonel Sherman as he dashed about, wearing his bright blue silver-laced uniform. He was the only one thus supplied—even General Houston did not have a complete uniform.

"Just then General Houston and two or three officers came along the line and our captain turned his horse and rode out a few steps to meet them. They did not halt but Houston said something to Karnes and I heard the Captain reply: 'Depend on that, General.' Houston had not gone far down the line when I saw him rein his horse, turn to the men, draw his sword and point toward the Mexican encampment. Immediately came the command, 'Forward, my brave men! Charge the enemy and give them hell.' At last we were really going into battle.

"We did not go off in a helter-skelter charge, as I have often heard related, but our gait for a short distance was a trot, our speed increasing as we neared the enemy. The music by which we marched upon the foe was the then familiar and popular melody, 'Will you come to the bower I have shaded for you,' and was played on a single fife and a badly battered drum. Here it might be added that except for the time when General Havelock marched to the relief of Lucknow to the music of 'Annie Laurie' this was, so far as I know, the only time in history troops were led into battle to the strains of a love song.

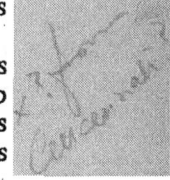

"One thing I particularly observed as the lines first moved forward to the attack. Our artillery—two small brass cannon, the famous 'Twin Sisters'—was drawn by horses, but when near the enemy the horses became excited and unmanageable and the guns then were drawn by men, two of whom I remember well, Clark Harmon and Tom Green. Both were powerful men. I have often heard Green (who later, by the way, became a famous Confederate general) tell how sore it made his muscles to yank the cannon around. Green and Harmon were the principal gunners. Ben McCulloch, afterwards a noted border chief and a gallant Confederate general, was in command of the guns. Young McCulloch, fresh from Tennessee, had arrived in Texas a little too late to join his neighbor, Davy Crockett, in the Alamo, but he attached himself to Houston's army to avenge, he said, his friends tragic death. And he did, for

"*The 'Twin Sisters' spoke mid the rifles' sharp crack,*
The clashing of swords and the yell,
Of men who fought on, but never turned back
Till the battle was won and won well.

"As we came in full view of the Mexican breastworks, the music changed to the lively strains of Yankee Doodle [38] but just at the moment something occurred far more inspiring and thrilling. Mud-spattered, and on foaming steed, the heroic Deaf Smith dashed up and along the lines, frantically waving an ax above his head, and shouted: 'Vince's bridge is gone! No escape, boys! Fight fast and hard!' and then wheeling, the gallant old scout ran ahead and over the barricade. His horse, exhausted, stumbled and fell, throwing the rider among the enemy. Smith quickly arose and drawing his pistol, attempted to shoot a Mexican who was about to run him through with a bayonet. For once the scout's trusty pistol failed to fire, but he hurled the

---

[38] I have conversed with a number of San Jacinto Veterans who verified Captain Taylor's statement, that the music was changed just at the moment of the attack, to the lively strains of "Yankee Doodle."

weapon at the head of his assailant. As the stunned Mexican staggered back Smith seized his gun and dispatched him. So, if it is worth anything to history, I can vouch for the fact that Deaf Smith began the fight and drew the first blood at San Jacinto.

"The Texan yell was the order to charge, and like a cyclone crashing through the forest, we went over the dirt and brush barricade without halting. A solid sheet of flame flashed from our rifles, and then, without waiting to reload, we bore down and closed in upon the surprised and frightened enemy with clubbed guns, pistols, and hunting knives. It was a hand to hand struggle; and now came the bloodstirring cry, 'Remember the Alamo! Remember Goliad!' Instantly the appeal was caught up and repeated with more and more feeling. It seemed to nerve every Texan to fight with greater desperation and to fire with deadlier effect.

"It is little wonder that Santa Anna, attempting to excuse himself for his inglorious flight from the field, afterwards wrote: 'So sudden and fierce was the enemy's charge that the earth seemed to move and tremble.'

"Just inside the breastworks my horse fell and I thought he was shot. But he quickly regained his feet, and after reloading my gun I mounted and dashed on into the thick of the fray. At this moment I saw Karnes kill a Mexican with his pistol and then throw the discharged weapon at another, knocking him over. As the Mexican was trying to scramble up, he was struck over the head with a rifle and killed.

"When we—I speak particularly of Karnes' company, as I could not see what was going on with the others—crossed the breastworks, all company formation and order was at an end. Every man was his own captain, fighting his own way with only one aim—to kill Mexicans. Orders given by commanding officers were drowned in the noise or little heeded. In fact, but little semblance of order existed after the fight began. It seemed that every fighter was transformed into a wild, furious beast with but one impulse, and that to slay. 'No me mates' (do not kill me), was heard on every side, but our men gave no heed to these appeals. They used their heavy sheath knives with deadly effect. Some used their guns as they would a club. The Mexican guns had bayonets, and these were seized in many instances and the Mexicans were run through with their own weapons.

"From the first onslaught the fight was fast and furious. And what a terrible scene! The yells of the infuriated Texans, the shouts of the confused Mexicans, and the crack of fire arms, making a veritable bedlam. Many of the terror-stricken Mexicans simply threw down their arms and begged for mercy. 'Me no Alamo! Me no Goliad!' was heard on every hand. But the appeals of the poor fellows were in vain. The slaughter went on with relentless fury.

"During the progress of the struggle, many acts of individual heroism and gallantry were displayed; and for one thing, it can be said that not one gesture of cowardice was displayed by a San Jacinto man. Dr. Motley, a young surgeon on Houston's staff, was about the first of our boys to fall. After receiving his death wound and with his dying breath he cheered his comrades on. This gallant martyr to Texan liberty was one of the signers of our Declaration of Independence, and his memory is perpetuated in the name of one of the counties of Texas.

"Perhaps the most conspicuous figure in the fight was the dauntless Captain Ware and his heroic band of eighteen select riflemen from the San Bernard. They were well to the front and under close fire, suffering more than some of the larger companies. One of the number, George A. Lamb, was killed and four others, sergeants Will Winters and Albert Gallatin, and privates Rector and Robinson, wounded. The ball which hit Gallatin first struck his powder horn, cutting through the shot pouch and entering the side, carrying the strap of leather into the wound. Captain Ware was wild and furious and when the charge was ordered he leaped to his place in front and shouted, 'Come on, boys.' It was almost a miracle that none of the balls hit the captain, for he was in the lead, standing in his stirrups, springing into the air and shouting at every jump.

"From the moment we set up our yell and opened fire there was consternation in the Mexican camp. The enemy was completely surprised. Most of the officers evidently were asleep as some of them were found shot while they reposed on their cots, and it was apparent that the Mexican soldiers were just preparing their evening meal, as their tables were left spread when the assault came. It was about four o'clock and to add to their confusion the western sun was shining directly in the enemy's face. General Houston said he purposely had timed the attack so the sun would be in the Mexicans' eyes.

"But the Mexicans were not cowards and for a time fought desperately. However, as the onslaught increased and the Texans became more desperate, the foe lost spirit and fell back, finally running toward the center of their encampment where their brave officers tried to rally them to their colors. It was here, in his heroic efforts to rally his troops that the brave Colonel Castrillion fell. But the rush was too fast for the Mexicans to escape the fury of the 'diablos tejanos' (Texas Devils). Our men were avenging the death of their friends in the Alamo and at Goliad, and everyone was determined to take full toll.

"The Mexican artillery was soon silenced. It was around the artillery park that the fiercest fighting and most desperate hand-to-hand struggles occurred; in fact, the greater number of the enemy were killed around their cannon. I could have walked over a large circle on their dead bodies. Here in this bloody angle the struggle was terrific, the Texans using their heavy hunting knives as cleavers, or wielded their guns as clubs to knock out the brains of the Mexicans. Here was the bloodiest battle scene on all the field.

"And now presented an exciting scene. In the midst of the melee and when the fighting was fiercest, I heard someone shout, 'Look! Look! Yonder goes old Santa! He's running away! Let's catch him.' Looking across the prairie, I saw a small body of gaily uniformed horsemen riding rapidly from the field. It was the Mexican chief and his body-guard, who, realizing that all was lost, was seeking safety in wild flight.

"It was the terrifying Texan yell and the headlong charges of our cavalry that so frightened the Mexicans and put them into wild flight. On our right the glorious Lamar commanded the cavalry and performed many acts of heroism, charging down upon the enemy and driving them before him. With him were such intrepid fighters as Walter P. Lane, Deaf Smith, Henry Karnes, Peter H. Bell, Wash Secrest, Olin Trask—as brave and determined men as ever rode in line of battle. His position brought him in front of Santa Anna, and it was the desperate charge of Lamar that caused the Mexican general to abandon his army and flee for life.

"Santa Anna was mounted on a coal black charger, which later proved to be the noted 'Old

Whip,' Allen Vince's fine stallion stolen by the Mexicans the day before. A few of Lamar's cavalrymen at once gave chase and soon the escort was overtaken and slain. But Santa Anna, being mounted on a swift steed, outdistanced his pursuers. Reaching the bayou and finding the bridge gone, he plunged into the mire and was unable to extricate himself. But the fugitive 'Napoleon of the West' managed to scramble out, and hid in the brush and high grass bordering the stream until night. Thus afoot and bewildered, he wandered around, but made little further progress toward escape. The manner in which he was captured the next day by a party of our scouts, will be told at another time.

"Once the order to charge was given and the furious fight began, all semblance of order had ceased. The respective commanders were simply unable to direct or control their men. Even the commander-in-chief himself was virtually as a private.

"Although wounded early in the action, the ball shattering his ankle and penetrating his horse, General Houston displayed unusual bravery and calmness throughout, as he rode here and there encouraging the men and endeavoring to direct operations. His wounded horse, covered with foam and blood, finally fell, but the general quickly remounted another and spurred forward into the thick of the fray shouting, 'Come on, my brave fellows. Your general leads you.'

"Houston's enemies accused him of cowardice at San Jacinto; that he was unduly excited, and that he became a hero by accident. I observed the general on the field several times during the fight, and I can say truthfully that in every instance and in every way, he appeared cool and collected. I can never forget his magnificent and commanding appearance as he dashed from point to point over the field. He certainly looked and acted every inch a military chieftain.

"It was the great Napoleon, I believe, who said 'quarter hours decide the destinies of nations.' And so it was at San Jacinto. The battle was soon won but the slaughter continued in the different directions until it was quite dark. It is said that the battle lasted only fifteen or twenty minutes. It seemed longer than that to me, but admitting the statement to be true, one can form some idea of the desperation of the boys when he considers the number killed in that brief time. General Almonte rallied a considerable number of his fleeing men and surrendered. These would have been killed had not our officers prevented their slaughter. They used every means to stop the killing of the panic stricken and fleeing Mexicans, but it was some time before the men gave any heed to their commanders.

"When the firing did cease our boys were wild with delight. General Houston rode over the field with blood dripping from his stirrup and tried to establish order by urging the men to get into line and fall back to camp. But he only met with good-natured raillery, whereup the general is said to have exclaimed, 'Boys, I like your courage, but damn your manners.'

"Finally a semblance of order was established and the men began to perform the duties assigned to them: caring for the wounded, collecting the guns, ammunition and camp equipage left strewn about the field. Dead Mexicans lay everywhere and in every position, some officers on their cots, enlisted men lay dead across the campfires, slain while preparing the evening meal. It was a gruesome scene I can never forget.

"The dead Mexicans were not buried—Santa Anna evinced no desire to have that done—but allowed them to remain where they had fallen. The Mexican prisoners were gathered together and placed under guard around a big campfire. A guard was placed around Santa Anna's tent, where the army chest was found. General Houston had all monies found turned in and it was then equally divided among the boys. But the men were so joyful over the great victory that they cared but little for the spoils. The murder of their friends had been avenged and Texas was free from tyrannical rule.

"Among other things discovered in the Mexican camp was a great quantity of tallow candles which were brought out and distributed among the men. The old fife and drum again played, 'Will you come to the bower,' and, lighting their candles, the boys began a wild dance, each holding in his hand a blazing candle, as he sang, yelled, and whirled around the big campfire. They were intoxicated with the joy of victory and kept up the revelry until a late hour.

"From the clear sky of that eventful night the stars actually seemed to shine brighter—as if taking cognizance of what had transpired.

> "The strife is o'er, the fight is done
> The field is gained, the battle won
> The close of day, the set of sun
> Sees Texas free, her race begun."

The 'Lone Star' of Texas arose in dim luster at Washington town, March 2nd, 1836. San Jacinto gave it effulgence—to shine with increasing radiance as the years roll by. It is the Star of Empire.

CHAPTER XIX

Tragedy and Humor Stalk the Field of San Jacinto

"The first day of a free Texas was a glorious one. As the sun arose on the morning following the battle it seemed to me to shine with more splendor; all nature appeared more radiant and beautiful; the fields of blue-bonnets lending an azure hue to the landscape, appeared even more brilliant and fragrant. We were all happy. By daylight the Texan camp and the nearby battle field was a scene of activity. Groups could be seen about the camp-fires, preparing roast beef—about all we had for breakfast; the boys were jesting and laughing as if on a holiday jaunt, others looking after their *hobbled* horses that had strayed out on the prairies; and some saddling up for a scout up the bayou.

"After breakfast men were seen all over the battle ground, gathering up arms, accoutrements, and articles of various kinds which the Mexicans had abandoned in their stampede the evening before, while some of the boys were amusing themselves by decorating the mules and horses with officers sashes, ribbons, and gold tinsels.

"I was told that a few days after the battle, a man was seen extracting the teeth of dead Mexicans, though the stench was something fierce. Be it known, however, that this enterprising fellow was not one of our comrades, but one of those who had flocked to the battlefield after the news of victory. He was a dentist from the 'States,' and was supplying himself with the necessary adjuncts of his profession. No one disturbed him in his gruesome work.

"All the boys lamented the escape of the 'big dog of the tan yard,' as they called Santa Anna, and scouts were soon planned to scour the country for the fugitive. Early on the morning of the 22nd, Si Bostick came to me and said he was going on a 'still hunt' with two or three fellows and asked me to go along. Bostick and I were perhaps the youngest lads in the army and we were the best of chums. We were comrades together at Gonzales, Conception, in the Grass Fight, and at the siege and capture of Bexar, and we were very close friends. But the lack of a suitable mount—my horse had been shot from under me in the battle—I declined to go. After the boys left I kept thinking that I might be missing some fine sport—I could imagine them flushing a covey of 'greasers' and chasing them across the prairies.

"The scouting party that captured Santa Anna was composed of Joel W. Robinson, A. H. Miles, Charles P. Thompson, Joseph Vermillion, and Siron R. Bostick, led by Color Sergeant James A. Sylvester, the gallant young man who bore the 'Liberty or Death' flag through the battle of San Jacinto, the only flag flown on the field by the Texans that day.

"In flushing the vicinity near Vince's Bayou, the Mexican general was discovered crouching in the tall grass along a small hollow. He was first sighted by Jim Sylvester who suddenly rode upon the fugitive. The Mexican had on a corporal's uniform and was bare-footed. Sylvester at once signaled his men scattered around some four or five hundred yards away, and as they began dashing up and flourishing their guns, Santa Anna became excited, and it was at that moment that he first gave the Masonic sign of distress. Both Sylvester and Robinson were Masons and they understood what 'them funny motions meant,' and this no doubt accounts for the fact that the captive was not killed on the spot.

"The captive was ordered to march ahead on

foot toward the camp, but soon he stopped and declared that because of his bare blistered feet he could go no further. Whereupon Miles drew his gun and threatened to fire if he didn't 'step along lively.' They proceeded some half a mile when the prisoner suddenly stopped and said: 'Señor, I cannot walk bare footed any further, even though you kill me.' Several of the boys leveled their guns and were ready to shoot, when Robinson interceded, saying, 'Don't kill the poor fellow.' He then reached down, took the hand of the prisoner and said, 'Get up behind me.' Si Bostick often said that he guessed that was about Santa Anna's closest call, a moment later he would have fired and the checkered career of the famous Mexican would have ended near the spot of his great downfall.

"Thus Santa Anna was captured and brought into the Texan army camp. As the party approached General Houston's headquarters, which was under a large live-oak tree, I hailed Bostick and asked: 'Si! Who have you got there?' 'Don't know Creed, but we thing he's a big buck.' This was only a few paces from the 'dead line' where the Mexican prisoners were being guarded. No sooner had Bostick spoken than I saw several of the prisoners salute and heard them say, 'Es el Presidente! Es nuestro General! It is the President! It is our general!' Hearing this I hastened to headquarters and I saw and heard everything that occurred in that great moment of our country's history.

"On reaching headquarters the captive quickly slid down from the horse and was immediately led to Houston. General Almonte was the first man to approach him and at once introduced him to General Houston, who, owing to his wound, did not rise to his feet, but did rise to a sitting posture and very cordially extended his hand which

SANTA ANNA BEFORE HOUSTON AT SAN JACINTO

Santa Anna grasped as if it were that of an old friend. I could not see that Santa Anna was unduly excited, though he appeared quite serious. He bore himself with an air of a fearless—I might say, defiant—man, although at that moment the boys, with fury depicted in their faces, were gathering from every quarter and it was with an effort that the guards held them back.

"I cannot recall all the conversation between the two generals; but that interview is of record, and a matter of familiar history. I do remember that Santa Anna did not appear 'shaky,' nor did he ask for an opiate. Meanwhile the crowd continued to gather, and threats, in an undertone, were heard on every side, and I believe that Santa Anna's being a Free Mason was all that saved him on that day. Houston, Sherman, and many others of our officers were Masons and while a number of them doubtless favored the execution of the red-handed monster, yet they were bound to observe their Masonic obligations. I offer this, however, as my opinion and this idea prevailed generally among the men. Comrade Bostick stood near Santa Anna, as if still guarding the captive, watching every movement and listening attentively to all that was said. 'Something seemed to give Santa Anna confidence all at once,' said Bostick, and I know now what it was. He and Houston were both Free Masons, and the prisoner made the sign of distress, which Houston, as a Mason, heeded. I was told that at the time by one of our men, who was a Mason also, and I am now certain it was the strong tie of fraternal brotherhood that saved Santa Anna's life.[39]

"One incident I distinctly remember. In the course of the interview, Santa Anna, casting his eyes about recognized Manchaca, who had so bravely

[39] Unpublished Reminiscences of Siron R. Bostick.

fought on the Texan side with Captain Seguin's Mexican company, and at once appealed to him for favor and kind treatment. Manchaca was a man of wit and ready repartee and with a sardonic smile and a twinkle of the eye, he drew his hand across his throat and exclaimed: 'Oh, yes! I know what you would do, if you had me as prisoner!' This attitude of the patriotic Manchaca, toward his countryman, of course, served to intensify the feeling against Santa Anna and he became more serious and somewhat agitated; and it was at this moment, as I have been reliably informed, that he gave the distress sign of a Master Mason.

"General Houston showed the distinguished prisoner the utmost consideration, even preventing the Texans from firing a salute celebrating the capture of the Mexican general; and this served to still further exasperate some of boys who were unfriendly to the Texas Commander and who were loudest in their demands for the Mexican captive's blood. Houston had Santa Anna's tent erected near his own, the Mexican general's bed with finest coverings, placed therein—the only bed at San Jacinto—but the fallen chief slept little that night. The Texans including General Houston, reposed on the ground, but they slept well and happy. Santa Anna was allowed to choose his body servants and to use all the furnishings of his fine marque.[40]

"Second only to Santa Anna, General Cos was the object of supreme contempt and hatred to the men, more especially to those who had witnessed the sacrifice of Ben Milam and other comrades in San Antonio the preceding December, and had witnessed

---

(40) In his "Manifesto" of the Texas campaign, addressed to his fellow citizens from Veracruz, May 10, 1837, Santa Anna says of General Houston:
"In all justice it must be confessed, however, that the Texan general, Sam Houston, is educated and is actuated by humanitarian sentiments. I am indebted to him for a treatment as decorous as the circumstances permitted while he was in Texas, and for my liberty after he returned from New Orleans where he went to have a wound received at San Jacinto treated."

his surrender. Cos had surrendered as a prisoner of war and had never been exchanged. By the violation of this parole he forfeited all claims to leniency and I believe to this day that he should have been marched out in front of the Mexican prisoners and shot.

"General Almonte was one of the most attractive men among the prisoners. He was a man of fine appearance, genial and highly educated. He had visited Texas a few years before the outbreak of hostilities and he remembered many of his captors whom he had met before and for each of these he had pleasant words. I had it from good authority that 'Almonte' was not his right name. I was told that his father was the insurgent priest who first raised the 'grito' for Mexican Independence in 1810. At one time later during the ensuing war Hidalgo and the lad, with a small escort, were riding along the highway, when suddenly they found themselves almost surrounded by the Spanish troops under Calega. Hidalgo, seeing capture inevitable, shouted to the boy, 'Al monte! Al Monte!' (To the hills! To the hills!) The boy fled as directed and was ever afterward known as 'Almonte.'

"One more little incident of San Jacinto and I will have done with my poor account of some of the things I saw there, although the event I am going to relate occurred a day or so after I left, but it was told to me by several of the boys who were eyewitnesses. A large amount of ammunition had been captured, among which were quite a lot of cartridges gathered up loose and piled in a heap not far from Santa Anna's tent, which was guarded by a sentinel in front and one in the rear. Tom Nail was on duty that day as guard at the rear of Santa Anna's tent and no man ever breathed that hated the Mexican chief more than Tom.

"By some means during the day fire got out in

the dry grass and reached the pile of cartridges with the result that there was a furious and prolonged explosion. It sounded like the continued rattle of musketry and produced quite an excitement in the camp. Hearing the uproar Santa Anna got the idea that there was an uprising of the prisoners and, rushing to the rear of his tent, he bent low to the ground and, raising the cloth, put his head out to see what was going on. Sentinel Nail was carrying a Mexican escopeta, with a fixed bayonet, and when he saw Santa Anna's head poked out, he made a vicious lunge at it with his bayonet which missing its mark, buried itself to the gun muzzle in the ground. Of course the general's head got back quicker than it came out, but until the day of his death Tom Nail cursed his ill luck in not pinning Santa Anna's head to the ground on that occasion.

"Strange to say our histories of Texas say little or nothing about the disposition of the Mexican dead at San Jacinto and the question is often asked if they were buried. As stated, they were not buried but left to decay where they fell. But the sequel proved that these carcasses should have been buried or burned. Dead Mexicans lay everywhere and in every position. It was a ghastly sight I can never forget. Santa Anna evinced no desire to have his slain men interred, and of course we Texans were not concerned about the final disposition of these unfortunate 'greasers.' The fact is that immediate burial of so large a number of corpses was rendered impracticable by the great fatigue which the Texans had endured, and by the care of the prisoners and captured army property.

"Soon the bodies, drenched by the heavy rains and heated by the burning sun, presented a fearful, most ghastly sight, swelling to enormous sizes and decaying with a revolting stench. No one, of course, wanted to engage in the gruesome work. The boys saying that they came to kill, but not to bury Mexicans, and it was jocosely suggested that a dead 'greaser' would turn to a mummy anyhow—that there was not vitality enough about them to cause decomposition; that at the Alamo and at Goliad our dead were burned, but that we would be more humane and leave the unfortunate Mexicans to rest in peace on the field.

"I have often heard the story of how a Mrs. McCormick, on whose estate the principal portion of the slain Mexicans lay, called at General Houston's headquarters and requested him to 'have them stinking Mexicans removed from her land.' The general, with mock seriousness, replied, 'Madam, your land will be famed in history as the classic spot upon which the glorious victory of San Jacinto was won. Here that last scourge of mankind, the arrogant, self-styled Napoleon of the West, met his fate.' 'To the devil with your glorious history!' the madam replied, 'Take off your stinking Mexicans.'

'No Buzzards or wolves came about them, and the odor exuding from the corpses which lay rotting south of our camp, became terrible, causing the army to move up to Harrisburg.[41]

"After the flesh rotted off, the cattle pawed over and chewed the bones to the extent that their milk and meat was unfit for use. The citizens of the vicinity then gathered up and buried the bones, all except the skulls, which could not be chewed. The skulls lay on the ground and some of them could be seen many years later. Some of them were carried away as souvenirs; but I never had any desire for such relics."

[41] Colonel Delgado, complaining of the treatment of himself and his fellow prisoners of war, says, "Still more intolerable was the stench arising from the corpses on the field of San Jacinto, which they (the Texans) did not have the generosity to bury, after the time-honored custom, regardless of their own health and comfort, and those of the surrounding country."

CHAPTER XX

From Camp-fire to Hearth-stone

"On the eve of the battle at San Jacinto, General Houston had made a short talk, telling us that if we fought hard and won victory we would all be 'captains.' The fighting was indeed hard, the result, a glorious victory that insured the independence of Texas from a powerful nation, and of course we all did feel like we were captains. The dictator of all Mexico was now an humble captive in our camp, the spoils of war were ours and our joy knew no bounds. But after a few days of carousing, gadding, and gossiping, the novelty of the situation wore off and we began to tire of idle camp life.

"Now that the campaign was ended and the Mexican army was overthrown, my thoughts were of peace, loved ones, and home; and so Josiah and I bid farewell to our comrades in camp, and went back to mother and the children. The gladsome news of the great victory had already reached them, and what a change! It would be impossible for me to tell how happy the folks were. Those were the happiest days of my life. The forests and prairies were in full green and looked inexpressibly lovely. The birds seemed to sing a new song of gladness and all nature appeared in holiday attire. In a few days we were all on the home-ward march, but the return trip was a very different one from the hurry-scurry runaway. Mother was as jovial as a girl at a ball and the children were enlivened by a spirit of gayety. The real secret was we were going back home. The Mexicans had been whipped and we had nothing to fear at their hands anymore.

"As we pushed forward the days seemed shorter and the distance ahead seemed greater than ever before. We had only a small stock of provisions—jerked beef, parched corn—but we didn't feel the pangs of hunger. The night after we crossed the Colorado floods of rain fell and we became thoroughly soaked, but we didn't mind the rain—we were going home. We overtook many other refugees who were returning home and they too, without exception were in high spirits. We expected to find nothing but ashes and a heap of ruins where we had left our homes and shelter, but now this could be borne with resignation since Texas was free and the Mexican power was forever broken. Under the protection of our own 'rule' and with the land at peace, we could soon rebuild our homes, replenish our herds, and as for the Indians we could cope with them.

"I think it was on the 10th or 12th of May that we reached home, late in the evening, and we found the house and the out-buildings intact, but the vandals had been there and little of value remained. Fires had been made in the yard, feathers were scattered about the premises and the bones of fowls scattered round told too plainly where mother's chickens had gone. Our rude furniture was broken and the few books she had left on the side-shelf were gone. The crib and the smoke-house were empty. The doors were broken from their wooden hinges. The festering remains of old 'Lep,' the faithful watchdog, were lying just inside the door of the dwelling. Whether he died defending the entrance or starved, or was killed and his body thrown there, will never be known.

"That night we repaired the old broken table and at supper we gathered once more around the festal board which was lightly burdened with a scant supply of dried beef, while our beverage was water—drunk from a Spanish gourd. But to us it was a joyful feast because we were at home.

Next morning our joy was increased when we found that some of our neighbors had returned, and two weeks later they gathered from far and near at our house and danced all night—we were celebrating our recent great victory in the manner of that day and time.

"We were happy, hopeful, and willing to work hard; now that we lived in our own free country. Privations were forgotten in the hopes of better times. We made a very good crop of corn that year although late in planting. Our stock, on the range, had not been molested to any great extent and it took us but a few years to regain what losses we had sustained in the great Runaway Scrape.

"After the War of Independence and the launching of the republic, frontier expansion began; and with that movement came more war—that long and bitter strife between the determined frontiersmen and the infuriated Indians for mastery of the country. Complete peace for Texas did not come for many a year. In this sanguinary struggle of half a century, the Comanches were the most warlike and troublesome. They were 'lords of the realm,' and were constantly swooping down from their mountain strongholds and depredating all along our exposed frontier. A Ranger force must be constantly maintained and men who were able and willing to campaign in that 'fast riding and hard fighting' troop were needed. Having tired of the environments and monotony of civil life, I determined to join the Rangers, and so mounting my best horse I rode down to Victoria and enlisted in Captain David E. Murphy's company. Shortly after this, learning that Captain Bird Lockhart's company of Rangers was under orders to go to San Antonio and wishing to revisit the scenes of my recent conflicts, I transferred to this troop. We immediately set out for Bexar and in due time arrived at the Alamo, whose walls and floors had recently been crimsoned with the blood of martyred comrades. The scene of desolation around the old fortress, the evidence of the terrible conflict, and the silence which seemed to brood over the scene of the late carnage, was indescribable. Strong men of our own company—men who had brothers or other relatives and friends who fell with Travis —wept as little children when they were shown dark red stains on the mute stones of this 'Thermopylae of Texas,' and there was none to give them comfort in their silent grief. At this time on a corner building near the Alamo appeared large charcoal pictures of Bowie and Crockett with their names beneath. Crockett was holding a long barreled rifle and Bowie was firing a pistol. Another drawing without any name, but with a drawn sword was no doubt intended for Travis, and still another of these caricatures may have been intended for Bonham.

"Historian Yoakum gives Colonel Seguin and his command the credit for having collected and buried the ashes of the Alamo victims. On the morning after Lockhart's company arrived orders were given to make search for the remains of the Alamo men in order that they might receive Christian burial. I claim to be one of the first to discover the spot where these martyrs to liberty were cremated. Near the Alamo we discovered a dim trail which lead us to the spot about one half or three-fourths mile northeast from the fortress. And what a sad sight! The heaps of burned bones told the story of Mexican cruelty. In a long row the bodies of the Texans had been stacked, first a layer of wood and inflammable substances, then a layer of men, and so on alternately until all the bodies had been prepared for the poorly arranged cremation, when the pile was ignited. The wood being shorter than the bodies, in many instances the skeletons remained only partially destroyed, which made more terrible the hideous sight.

"I reported the discovery to Captain Lockhart who had the remains carefully collected, and placed in a large, neat, black coffin, with the names of Bowie, Travis, Crockett, and Bonham, engraved upon a metallic tablet and attached to the inside of the lid. A solemn procession was then formed and the coffin was tenderly borne to the Military cemetery where appropriate ceremonies were performed and orations delivered, after which the remains of the immortal heroes of the Alamo were buried with military honors.

"I have found that writers on Texas history do not agree in their reports of that funeral. In a published letter written by Juan N. Seguin, in 1878, he says that he collected the remains of the Alamo victims and placed them in an urn and buried them near the altar in San Fernando Cathedral. Several years ago my attention was called to an account of the obsequies as published in the 'Texas Register' in 1837. Both of these accounts are at variance with the facts. It is well known that Seguin took command at Bexar on the retirement of the Mexican troops shortly after the battle of San Jacinto. The remains of the Alamo victims were not collected and buried until February 25th, 1837. Why did Seguin wait ten months before gathering up the charred remains of his old comrades and give them Christian burial? The truth is, Colonel Seguin took no steps toward this matter until the arrival of our company, and then showed his indifference in divers ways. He seemed not to know even where the heaps of these remains were and made no effort to aid us in locating them, and when they were at last found, collected and prepared for burial, no one thought of consulting Seguin as to how or where they should be laid to rest.

"The account in the *'Texas Register'* is far-fetched and overdrawn. The only music I heard was that of a bugle. There was a procession, but on a scale quite humble as compared to that recorded by the *Register*. At the grave in the old Military cemetery we heard speeches—I do not remember who the orators were—the coffin was then lowered and three volleys fired over the open grave. Others to the contrary, these are the facts—perverted statements should not mar a country's history nor be used in eulogizing its heroes.

"Delving thus far into the past and speaking of this memorable event brings vividly forth many memories of stirring scenes of the long ago. 70 years have rolled away since that day I rode into Bexar and assisted in collecting and performing the last sad rites over those immortal heroes; and though in point of time far removed from the occurrences of that unparalleled struggle and heroic defense, yet as the scenes of the terrible conflict pass as in panoramic review, aged as I am, my old blood warms and courses through my veins; with quickening flow, I feel the stirring impulses of youth and would again heed the call to arms. But again I reflect, though time has dealt gently with me and I am spared to the living from that chivalric era of fierce strife and carnage, I well know my life is drawing to a close, that I am fast approaching the border of another, an unknown land, and that ere long I must cross over and join my old comrades in arms.[42]

"And now the drama closes, the curtain comes down, and my story ends."

[42] Captain Creed Taylor died at his home near Noxville, Kimble Co., Texas, December 27, 1906. He had lived to a venerable age—past the hundredth milepost in life's journey. His exact age was not clearly known, and the dates of his birth and of his arrival in Texas were merely conjectural even with himself. He informed the author that the only family record kept by his father's family was that in an old Bible which was lost in the "Runaway Scrape" just before the battle of San Jacinto.

Date Due			
NOV 2 - '50			
OCT 3 1 '55			
MAY 2 - '62			
MAY 25 '62			
MY 28 '64			
OC 19 '67			
MY 5 '68			
MY 22 '68			
OC 14 '68			
OC 28 '68			
NO 11 '68			

Tall men with long rifles ; the
976.4 T21

3 1927 00129743 8

976.4
T21